AF515789

365 WAYS TO SAVE THE ENVIRONMENT

Om Books International

Reprinted in 2025

Corporate & Editorial Office
A-12, Sector 64, Noida 201 301
Uttar Pradesh, India
Phone: +91 120 477 4100
Email: editorial@ombooks.com
Website: www.ombooksinternational.com

Sales Office
107, Ansari Road, Darya Ganj
New Delhi 110 002, India
Phone: +91 11 4000 9000
Email: sales@ombooks.com

Author: Nita Ganguly
Edited by: Anjana Saproo

ISBN: 978-93-5276-095-4

Printed in China

10 9 8 7 6 5 4 3

Contents

Preface

Change is inevitable. We all know that the environment is dynamic…it's bound to change. But this change is supposed to be gradual, smooth and constant. Like the tortoise, it should be slow and steady, giving enough opportunity to living organisms to adapt and evolve, in order to survive. But if this natural dynamic process gets accelerated and aggravated to an extent that keeping pace with the change is not possible for organisms, the results can be catastrophic and perhaps fatal.

Compared to the total time of the existence of the human race, the short period of post-industrialisation has seen man suppressing the need to preserve the environment in the name of development.

We need to focus on three aspects that have had the greatest impact on our environment:

1) Population explosion, leading to an increase in demand and supply, especially of food and water, has had a direct impact on the depletion of natural resources, increasing pollutants and toxic wastes, causing dramatic ecological degradation and changes.

2) Industrial revolution is always seen as advancement, development, prosperity. However, its consequences of increased pollution, overuse of natural resources like water, and other fallouts, has dramatic consequences for the environment.

3) The third and the most dramatic aspect is our way of thinking …our attitude! It's such a powerful tool, that if we use the right attitude now, it is not too late to mend the damage we have caused our planet, and save the only home that we all share - THE EARTH - from crossing dangerous limits and tipping points.

I dedicate this book to:

My husband, Dr (Lt. General Retd.) Manomoy Ganguly,VSM, who has always encouraged me to take up new challenges, supported me in all endeavours and inspired me to be who I am today. A true green crusader at heart who practices what he preaches…. My Green HERO!

Nita Ganguly

Educator, Author, Climate Leader and a Mentor.

1. Designs from Nature

There is an abundance of multi-functional design tools available to us in nature. Take a simple tree, for instance. The leaves are part of the crown that provides shade. They are also the food factories, which generate energy. The network of numerous underground roots helps support the tree. The bark serves as a protective layer for the more delicate inside wood of the tree and cools the moving water beneath the surface. Imagine imitating nature's simple and effective strategies to build beautiful spaces, buildings, streets and townships. This would go a long way in saving resources and sourcing energy that is resilient and sustainable.

2. How Does Nature Self-cool?

The bark is the tough, flexible armour, the life support system and the face of the tree. Each species has its unique bark pattern, often distinctive enough to identify the tree. It is the breathable surface that keeps the trunk and the water moving inside, nice and cool. The rough texture of the bark alternates between the shade, which is cooler, and the hot, sunny area. Dark and light surfaces absorb and give off heat to create a movement of air, thus removing heat from the bark surface. Similar alternating dark and light patterns can be seen on some animals' bodies. Take the African Zebra with its prominent black and white stripes. As these stripes heat up at different rates, they create a gentle breeze over the Zebra's body, cooling it down as it basks in the sun. Our buildings can support similar structures and colours that help keep the right temperature.

3. Nature Mitigates Flooding

We are living in a warmer world, where sea levels are rising and the numbers of storms and hurricanes have increased. Flood damage is huge. Previously, forests were able to help in reducing floods. They were natural absorbers of rainwater. When rainwater fell on the leaves of trees and plants, it would not fall directly on the ground. It dripped slowly on the forest ground and hence prevented floods.

But these forests have been systematically destroyed and cut down to make way for the construction of buildings and sealing water bodies. Water has to go somewhere.

How can our cities prevent flooding by learning from nature?

There are various solutions like reinvesting in wetlands and floodplains, and laying permeable pavements that can absorb rainfall. Other solutions include growing rooftop gardens. Urban environments should work hand in hand with nature.

4. Green Travel Trails

Designing a trail walk for nature lovers to follow the trail of animals that migrate daily or on a seasonal basis for food, shelter or to propagate is an exciting experience. Stick to marked trails to avoid harming native plants and consider taking a bag to pick up trash along your journey. As a responsible eco-traveller, you can help to improve the natural environment by promoting the well-being of the local habitat. Becoming a more responsible traveller is the best way to ensure your adventures don't damage the planet. Remember the old environmental saying, 'Take only pictures, leave only footprints'.

5. Power of a Click!

You see something fascinating, you immediately want to capture it in your mind.... Ahm! You use your phone camera these days. It's to share and convey messages, suggestions, or even point out environmental issues that we come across at the click of a button, thanks to the inbuilt camera in phones.

Mobile photography is awesome and there are thousands of camera apps available on smartphones. So take a journey through mobile photography and become an amateur eco-warrior for our planet Earth. Maybe the photographs taken by you can change our perspective of looking at issues. Or maybe it can motivate someone to BE THE CHANGE.... or bring in another green revolution!

6. Halt! Wildlife Crossing Ahead!

Every year, millions of animals die all over the world while crossing roads as they are hit and run over. These are the man-made roads that cross their jungle path, which they have been following for generations in search of food, migration and survival. They cannot change their course only because we decided to build roads. If roads can be built, so can crossing structures for the animals like tubes, tunnels, bridges, overpass, underpass, etc. This would be similar to the zebra crossings or the overpass bridges built for pedestrians. If we all decide to build wildlife crossing structures for the animals they can cross our roads safely. Animals don't understand country borders! Many cities have built wildlife crossings to help save the dwindling population of many species.

7. Not so Cool!

Many people put the air conditioner on at 21°C or colder as the summer heat sets in, and then cover themselves with blankets as it gets too cold. This wastes resources by burning electricity and causes health issues too.

The normal human body temperature is typically between 35°C to 37°C. The body can tolerate temperatures ranging from 22°C to 39°C. Running the AC at 21°C or below, lowers the body temperature and the person starts shivering involuntarily. This affects blood circulation. The AC stops us from sweating, which means our bodies don't get rid of the bad stuff, making us more likely to fall ill. Keep the AC at 25 degrees Celcius, run the fan and ventilate the room with fresh air regularly. It saves money and is great for your health.

8. Bottle Lights

Think of inexpensive and energy-efficient lights without turning on a single switch in a dark room. Is that possible? Yes. People in poor communities who could never see the light of day in their homes are now using simple technology to light their homes. You can do this too!

Let's experiment! All you need is a soda bottle. Fill it with water, a little chlorine, and then cap it. Remember to carry out this experiment under the supervision of an adult. This simple technology has many benefits. It provides much-needed light to people. Moreover, it gives a new life to used bottles which would have ultimately ended up as garbage. You can also save money and resources in this way.

9. The Useful Banyan Tree

Sadiman, a poor farmer from Bali, Indonesia, realised how serious the water crisis had become in the barren hills of Gendol, which had suffered deforestation and fires between the '60s to the '80s. To make rubber sap the tree sucks in water from the ground, yet no sap was formed. The lush green forest had turned barren. Sadiman took it upon himself to BE THE CHANGE and for 20 years, he alone planted and looked after the trees that stored underground water. He grew clove tree seedlings and traded expensive clove seeds for banyan seeds. People laughed at him for planting 'useless banyan seeds'. But he knew that these TREES PRODUCE WATER. Today, villagers have access to water in the form of streams and rivers because of one man who fought famine, one seedling at a time.

10. The Wonder Super Crops in the Era of Climate Change

Imagine producing superfood grains that are not only tasty but packed with rich, healthy vitamins, minerals and fibre. They are also cheap to produce. These super crops can grow in any type of soil, and use very little water. Like most grasses, their fibrous roots are good for the soil. Hardy crops like these can survive higher temperatures and don't need fertilisation. They also help farmers beat climate change. So, eat delicious wonder crops like MILLETS and help keep soils healthy.

11. Household Pollutants

Everybody checks the price tag before buying a product. But how many of us check the label of a product and find out what ingredients are used in making these? What about cleaners, paints and solvents, lawn and garden care products, automotive products, pool chemicals, even health and beauty aids? Are they really safe for us and our environment? If these products have chemical pollutants in them, then they are capable of releasing contaminants during their use in our daily life. Studies indicate that indoor air quality is far worse than that of outdoors because homes, for the purpose of energy efficiency, are made somewhat airtight. Moreover, household pollutants are trapped inside homes causing further deterioration of indoor air quality. Many commonly used household products in these categories release toxic chemicals. Some manufacturers claim to introduce green products. They make tall claims such as that the use and disposal of these are not a burden on the environment. To find out the truth all it requires is to do a Google search on the ingredients mentioned on the label or switching to a more reliable product that has nothing to hide.

12. Alternatives to Common Household Products

Air refresher: The air is fresh outside and you just need to open the windows to ventilate. To scent the air, use herbal bouquets, pure vanilla on a cotton ball, or simmer cinnamon and cloves.

Drain opener: Add 1 tablespoon baking soda into the drain and then slowly pour 1/3 cup white vinegar to loosen clogs. Use a plunger to get rid of the loosened clog. Prevent clogs by pouring hot boiling water down drains once a week using drain strainers, and not pouring grease down drains.

Fabric softener: Use 1/4 to 1/2 cup of baking soda during the rinse cycle.

Furniture polish: Mix 1 teaspoon of lemon oil and half liter of mineral oil and rub with a damp cotton cloth.

Insecticides: Wipe houseplant leaves with soapy water.

Laundry bleach: Use borax on all clothes or 1/2 cup of white vinegar and rinse water to brighten dark clothing.

Mothballs: Place cedar chips or blocks in closets and drawers.

It is best to switch to homemade, multi use, multipurpose Bio-Enzyme that can replace any toxic chemical used in the kitchen, toilets, floors and even in personal grooming.

13. Eco-friendly Packaging Is the Way Forward

Plastics are cheap to manufacture and have many uses. They are made from materials that are damaging to the environment. On burning, they give out toxic gases. Single-use plastics are thrown away after one use. They do not break down in the soil. Our 'disposable' lifestyle means more than 8 million tons of plastic are dumped into the oceans every year, killing birds and marine animals. In some instances, this plastic mountain would be bigger than Mount Everest! Thus, using reusable bags is a step forward. It's time to switch to a traditional packaging material like glass storage jars that are both reusable and recyclable. Wrapping paper made of up-cycled cardboard and blow-up air pillows made of recycled material are another great eco-alternative Corn-starch packaging, using mushroom roots, and seaweed packaging, are other exciting ways of getting eco-friendly.

14. Danger Ahead!

Plants and animals are very sensitive to pollution and global warming. In extreme cases, entire species gets wiped out from the face of the Earth. These are called 'indicator species' and they warn humans of changes to the environment before it is too late. Amphibians like frogs and toads live in two environments- land and water- and they make good indicator species. Their thin skin allows them to breathe when in water. This thin skin also absorbs many pollutants in its surroundings. The presence or absence of these frogs tells us a lot about the health of our environment. Perhaps they will help us save the day!

15. Control Pests Naturally

Natural biological pest controllers exist in nature where plants and animals act as natural enemies of pests. Birds, lady beetles, and lacewings act as pest eaters. Gliding birds eat hundreds of insects, like mosquitoes, beetles and moths.

Did you know that ladybugs are considered to be a symbol of good luck and farmers love them because they eat plant-eating pests? A single ladybird can gobble up 5000 aphids in its year-long life!

Don't panic the next time you find a spider sneaking up on you with all those legs and scary-looking fangs. Spiders give us free biological pest control services. They're ready to eat pests the moment their tasty favourites arrive and get entangled in their silky web!

16. Breath of Fresh Air

Did you know that the yolk and the white of an egg contain all the nutrients to produce a perfect chick? Oxygen is needed to complete this process. Have you ever wondered how a developing chick breathes in oxygen, while growing inside a sealed egg shell for 21 days?

Imagine an egg shell as having holes in it. Well, actually, egg shells do. To catch sight of them, just magnify the egg shells a thousand times, and you can find the calcium carbonate crystals that make up the shell. There are hundreds of tiny holes on the shell. These holes allow the exchange of oxygen-rich air to flow in and carbon dioxide gases to flow out.

But irresponsible human activities have turned this refreshing air into polluted air. Continual exposure to air pollution will reduce the population in bird communities.

17. Poop! Go the Eco-friendly Way

About 18 billion diapers are bought, used and thrown into landfills yearly. They decompose slowly over many decades contaminating the surrounding air, water and soil.

Single-use diapers are designed to be thrown away because it is difficult to sort the plastic from the biodegradable waste.

Basic cloth diapers are the most environmentally friendly option and can be used between 50 to 100 times before disposal. There are other environmentally–friendly diapers made from natural materials like cotton, hemp or bamboo, etc. These are free from chemicals, latex and plastic. They take less than a year to decompose, making them environment–friendly!

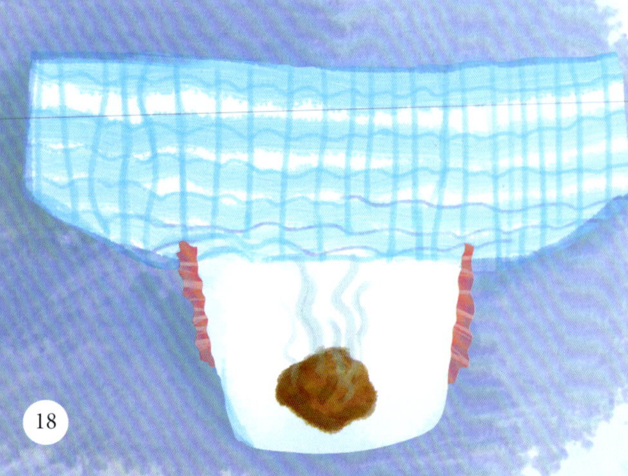

18. Follow the Toilet Rhyme

Are you familiar with a toilet rhyme that goes like this? "If it's yellow, let it mellow. If it's brown, flush it down." Well, it's just a reminder to save water after using the toilet.

On an average, people use the toilet 6 to 10 times a day using a minimum of 6 liters of treated water. That is a huge amount of wasted water.

Leaving pee in the toilet may be gross and yucky. But each flushing shoots an invisible 'toilet plume' into the air, spreading many germs. So next time you visit the toilet, use the rhyme and flip the lid of the pot down when not in use.

19. Grey to Black

Waste water from showers, baths and hand washbasins is called grey water. Black water is the waste water from the toilet. Black water is contaminated with disease-carrying bacteria.

Most bathrooms have pipes making tap water available to all facilities. When grey water is allowed to be discharged into sewers, it is wasted, as it can be converted into water for flushing the toilets. With minor changes in plumbing, grey water can be re-used to flush toilets. This will reduce wastage and save money in the long run.

20. Consumer's Choice

How do you choose a product? Is it based on word of mouth? Or do you listen to advertisements? Would you, for example, buy shampoo in bars or in bottles? Which of these do you think is better for the environment?

Homemade shampoos do not need packaging. But buying a ready-made product will require heavy packaging, including harmful plastics.

Instead, why not buy shampoo bars which are made of natural ingredients like oils? They smell nice and are better for the skin.

Plastic shampoo bottles are bad for the environment. Bought in bulk, there is further addition of plastic wraps to the bottles.

Take a look at the ingredients listed on the back of shampoo bottles. These are mostly harmful chemicals!

Using natural shampoos without plastic packaging benefits our hair and planet Earth.

21. Coconut Husk

The coconut husk is a protective cover. This is often thrown away before eating the coconut. But the husk has multiple uses. It can be turned into a value-added fuel source that is easily available and cost-effective in replacing traditional fuel sources like wood, or coal in power plants.

Burning coconut husk in rooms before bedtime repels mosquitoes. The smoke produced from burning is harmless as it is a natural product.

Coconut husk can be used as a planter. It will then slowly release its nutrients into the herbs and flowering plants growing in it.

Various household products such as carpets, coir, ropes, pots and others can be made from coconut husk.

22. Green Tender Coconut Delight!

Planters are containers where you can grow your favourite flowers, fruits or vegetables, even if you don't have much space. It creates a unique garden to your home in different shapes, sizes, colours and materials.

Traditional planters consist of materials that are not always good for the environment. Reusing natural earthy materials reduces waste and looks exceptional.

Take a tender coconut for instance. People usually throw away the outer green shell. Yet, any plant can be grown in it, by simply filling the cavity with soil. The fresh fibrous interior of the green coconut helps plants to grow well, as it holds moisture. Fill it with garden soil and sow a seed or place your plant. Drill or pierce holes in the shell first to create excellent plant holders. Why not hang them on trees, where they double up as bird feeders?

So next time you relish tasty coconut drink, bring the shell home and grow your favourite plant in it!

23. Sick Building Syndrome

Headache, dizziness, nausea, irritation and dryness in the sensory organs, dry cough, difficulty in concentration, and other allergies may plague you inside your home. You may feel better as soon as you leave your building.

The complaints may be localised in a particular room or zone, or may be widespread throughout the building.

Vacuum regularly to remove dust. Change the air filters every couple of months or when required. Set the right humidity. Get the air tested for indoor moulds and fungus. Change lights as needed. Place indoor plants that are known to absorb harmful fumes and remove toxins that trigger the symptoms. These are some of the steps that can be taken to reduce the harmful effect on the body.

24. Blue Light Harms

We are surrounded by blue light everywhere now. Computer screens, electronic notebooks, tablets, smartphones, fluorescent lights, LED lighting and other electronic digital devices; all emit significant amounts of blue light which is harmful.

Light at night is part of the reason why so many cannot sleep. It is best to TURN IT OFF, straight from the main switch.

Doing this has two benefits; First, there is a health benefit, as you get a good night sleep in a dark room. Second, your electricity bill goes down too, along with your carbon footprint.

So a simple act can save you and the Earth.

25. Be a Traveller, not a Tourist

A truly responsible traveller enjoys his travelling in the best possible way, with local people.

Here's what you can do to save the environment while travelling:

1. Pack light to save money on baggage fees. It also increases travel fuel-efficiency.
2. Pack quick-drying clothes that can be worn multiple times during your trip.
3. Save water and re-use towels for multiple days.
4. Save energy by switching off all electrical appliances before going out.
5. Every time housekeeping staff cleans the room they use harsh chemical cleaning supplies, electricity for vacuuming and detergents for washing bed linens. Try using the "Do Not Disturb" sign on the door when you feel the room can do without these housekeeping services.
6. Reduce- Reuse- Recycle as far as possible. Use just one bar of soap for both the sink and shower. Carry a non-disposable water bottle and refill it as and when required instead of buying plastic water bottles. Return brochures and maps once you're finished using them.

26. Plug the Food Wastage

Between one-third and one-half of all food produced globally is wasted or lost along supply chains every year. This impacts climate change. However, there is wastage of food at the consumer's end due to excess buying. This is often influenced by large portioning and package sizes in cash-and-carry stores that offer bulk discounts. Wastage also takes place due to confusion over labels showing best before and best use by date. Finally, food is wasted in homes due to discounts offered on bulk buying, poor storing practices and lack of proper refrigeration, etc. The way forward is to organise collaborate, take initiative to identify and distribute the food that could be potentially wasted, to the needy.

27. Powerful Duckling

Ducks love water. These birds are also called "waterfowl" because they are normally found in places like marshes, oceans, rivers, ponds, and lakes. Similarly, temporary lakes are also formed around deep green paddy fields largely immersed in water. Since water is common to both, integrating the two things makes sense. Rice-duck farming is a technique followed in many parts of the world and is an especially suitable resource for poor farmers to produce organic rice at a low cost.

In this technique, ducklings are released in the field after 10-20 days of rice transplantation right up to the time of flowering.

The continuous movement of ducks in the rice field strengthens the roots and also increases the availability of nutrients like nitrogen, phosphorous and potash to the rice crop.

This integrated rice-duck farming technique helps to reduce global warming.

28. Azolla, Loach Join the Powerful Duckling

Some Japanese farmers have developed a technique whereby they integrated organic Rice-duck farming along with the Azolla-loach farming bio-system.

Azolla is a thick-living carpet-like plant that helps prevent mosquitoes from laying eggs in the water. Loach is a bottom-feeding fish. When the farmers integrate the properties of Loaches and Azolla along with the duck waste in the water, they can harvest different organic products like rice, fish, duck meat and eggs. This process boosts the farmers' incomes.
The Azolla plants can later be harvested for animal feed.

These techniques reduce the farmer's workload as well as environmental damage, and increase food production.

29. Non-native Plants Cause Damage

Ask your elders if they recall reading articles in newspapers about the increase in asthmatic attacks, especially during the pollen season. One of the things responsible for this is the Mesquite tree, also called 'Vilayti Kikar'. They look quite similar to the Indian Kikar trees but are poles apart in behaviour. The 'Vilayti Kikar' were brought by the British to help grow trees in the desert wastelands of western India. Over time, these grew and caused a lot of damage to our environment.

These trees caused native plants to die out. This in turn killed the many local animals who ate the Indian Kikar trees for food.

These thorny mesquites can grow to be either shrubs or trees with very deep roots reaching a depth of almost 200 feet down into the soil. Thorny mesquites have very long roots and cause groundwater to dry up. Chopping them doesn't kill these trees. Their roots help the plants to grow back very quickly.

So, it's vital to study a non-native plant first before introducing it into a foreign environment.

30. 'Enemy's Enemy Is A Friend'

Food is essential for life processes to carry on. Plants make food by mixing carbon dioxide and water in the presence of sunlight. If any one of these ingredients is missing, they will go hungry.

Survival of the fittest is a law of nature. Living creatures are constantly competing with each other in order to survive. Based on this, scientists have identified a few varieties of both exotic as well as native vines and climbers that are doing a pretty good job in handling the invasive Mesquite menace. So without chopping trees, which is prohibited by law, these natural enemies of Mesquite are keeping a check on them from spreading and harming native trees.

As the old saying goes, 'Enemy's enemy is a friend indeed.'

31. Fermented Foods

Fermenting is an ancient technique of preserving food. Fermented foods are rich in beneficial probiotics and have been associated with a range of health benefits — from better digestion to stronger immunity. They have many other functions such as adding new flavours and textures to food, extending the shelf life of foods, and providing an environment for probiotics to grow and reproduce. Fermented foods are becoming more popular, and one can find most of these at regular supermarkets. However, making one's own fermented foods and customising them to your taste will most definitely assure quality and reduce the carbon footprint.

32. Cool Pavements

We usually wear light clothes in summer as they are better at reflecting sunshine and keeping us cool. Dark clothes absorb sunshine and keep us warm, making them perfect for winters.

This principle can be applied to cooling pavements which are traditionally black in colour. A dark-coloured asphalt absorbs between 80 and 95 percent of the Sun's rays, heating up not just streets but the entire surrounding area. The same pavements coated with light-coloured solar reflectors help to reflect solar rays so that less heat is actually absorbed, cooling and preserving the road and the surroundings.

Cool pavements can reduce the heat of the surface by as much as 10-15 degrees and help in improving air quality by neutralising smog. By cooling the air, lighter coloured asphalt can also help prevent heat-related illnesses and deaths.

Solar reflective surfaces glow at night, thus lowering the energy usage needed to light streets and parking lots when the Sun starts to set. These also improve night visibility and hence take care of safety.

The environmental benefits of cool pavements are priceless!

33. Zero Garbage Target

Have you ever wondered where the waste generated in our homes goes? It goes to the municipal bin. We must handle the garbage we create with responsibility. We can try to reach the 'Zero Garbage Target' by minimising the waste going into the municipal bin.

Two positive attitudes are a must:

- First, reduce waste.
- Second, realise that what we call garbage or waste is in fact a RESOURCE kept in transit bins (what we call dustbin) waiting to be reused and recycled.

This resource can be segregated into its respective transit bins for subsequent usage. Maybe you can start by implementing a three-bin system in your school. Choose appropriate colours for your bins like — RED, BLUE and GREEN.

In the RED bin you could place all non-biodegradable waste like plastic, polybags, aluminium foil, glass, and metals. This waste cannot be recycled on the school premises.

In the BLUE bin place paper which is unsoiled and used on both sides.

In the GREEN bin put all biodegradable materials from the kitchen, canteen and garden which can, in turn, be used for composting.

34. Green Bin: a Hole(y) Bin

Make your own Green Bin. You will need the following:

1. Biodegradable kitchen waste (cut into smaller pieces)

2. Bin: Large plastic bucket (3 feet high) with holes drilled on all sides as well as the base of the bin for aeration and drainage.

3. Fibres: Straw / coconut fibre/ twigs /sugar cane fibre /cooler pads/ peanut shells (locally available materials).

4. Garden black soil.

5. A lid (with holes) to cover the bin (not airtight).

Steps:

1. Get the bin ready with holes on all sides.
2. Layer the bin with the following materials:

   1st layer: place in fibres, less than a foot.

   2nd layer : sprinkle a layer of garden soil.

   3rd layer: keep adding your daily kitchen waste.
3. Mix the above from time to time if required.
4. Once the bin is full, layer it with fibre-like dry leaves and cover with a lid.
5. Leave for 3 to 4 months or till done.
6. Meanwhile prepare a new bin and continue the composting process.

Tips:

a. Sprinkle water only if required, depending on the moisture content of the compost. (generally not required for kitchen waste)

b. If there is a pungent smell, sprinkle the pit with a handful of dry coarse soil.

c. For compost pits kept in a balcony or small enclosures. Avoid adding: cooked food, non-vegetarian food, sweets or oil into the bin.
(Not applicable for underground / walled pits).

d. Besides the regular biodegradable kitchen waste, you can also add onion peels, raw egg shells, and brewed tea leaves in the bin.

35. Poison for One, Portion for Another

Vines, creepers and climbers are weak-stemmed plants and cannot grow straight up without support.

At the same time, some of these species have high medicinal value like:

- Bougainvillea: This is a traditional healer known for its anti-inflammatory properties.
- Rubber vine: The fruits of this vine are rich in vitamin C.
- Geloi (Tinospora cordifolia): This plant is used to treat liver diseases.
- Makora (Jackal jujube): This is good for treating stomach aches.
- Asian bushbeech (Gmelina asiatica): This plant is used as a blood purifier.

36. Live Fence

Live fences are boundary walls made of lines of trees, shrubs, creepers, and climbers that are planted close all around houses, buildings, farms or fields. They have their own advantages. They add beauty and provide privacy and protection against other humans, cattle, and wildlife. They act as windbreaks, provide shade, control dust and provide food for pollinating bees and other insects. They propagate greater species diversity and biological density.

37. The Young Green 2.2 Billion

The Earth changes its nature slowly, year after year, and most of the changes are too insignificant for us to actually feel. But today, we do see and feel the obvious impact of environmental catastrophes happening all around us.

But we need to look within before blaming others for climate change. Yes, it's YOU who could be the most powerful green crusader in the war to save planet Earth. Today, in 2021, our population stands at 2.2 billion; imagine our force, if all of you join to form one strong green — The YOUNG GREEN 2.2 BILLION. Then you can do wonders and set an example for others to follow, and carry the message for generations to come.

38. The Power of the Young Green Billion

Imagine what could happen if you convince your families to:

- replace old appliances with energy-star models.
- replace incandescent bulbs with LEDs.
- turn off their cars for just ten minutes a day while waiting in traffic or elsewhere.
- recycle 50% of everything recyclable.
- say NO to plastic.

These efforts would go a long way to saving our environment.

39. Kitchen Pots and Pans

Do you know that non-stick pans can kill a bird? Teflon-coated and other non-stick cookware, if heated to high temperatures, is acutely toxic to birds.

Materials such as Teflon, BPA plastics, melamine, and aluminium are commonly found in everyday kitchenware products, yet have been tied to disturbing health issues.

BPA plastics are neurotoxic so avoid cooking in these plastics right away. Even the hard plastic melamine dishes have cancer-causing chemicals that leach into your food. Aluminium has been linked to brain disorders. It is a soft, highly reactive metal and must be used with caution.

The good news is that there are many safer alternative materials that include: glass, high grade stainless steel, ceramic dishware with lead-free glaze. Other dependable food-safe options like cast iron, earthen pots, bamboo or wood containers, have been the old-fashioned cookware choices.

40. Organic Way to Get Rid of Powdery Mildew

Powdery mildew is a fungal disease. The fungus thrives in warm, humid environments. The mildew forms spores that spread through wind, insects, and water, which carries the disease to other plants.

Simple ingredients like milk, baking soda, vinegar, garlic can help to tackle the white powdery mildew. Let's find out how to use them without polluting the environment:

• Milk: Milk and/or whey (which is the watery part of milk that remains after the formation of curds) is more effective at killing powdery mildew than chemical fungicides. Mix 60 parts water with 40 parts milk or whey, and spray onto the affected plants twice a week. You can even use whole milk without dilution for a strong effect.

• Baking soda: The healing power of baking soda is tremendous. It is better to use a preventative treatment than a fungicide. Mix 1 tablespoon of baking soda and 1/2 teaspoon liquid hand soap with about 4 litres of water. Spray once a week with only freshly prepared solution in the absence of direct sunlight to get the best results.

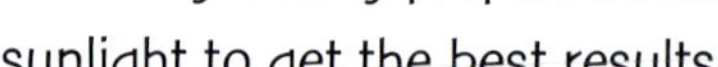

41. More Natural Ways to Get Rid of Powdery Mildew

There are other natural ways to get rid of mildew.

- Vinegar: An apple cider vinegar solution can remove fungus, bacteria and pesticides found on plants. One needs to take care not to make the mixture too strong as the acidity of the vinegar can burn plant leaves. Mix 4 tablespoons of apple cider vinegar (5% solution) with 4 litres of water. Spray every three days.

- Neem oil is powerful enough to kill powdery mildew in less than 24 hours. This oil is a great preventative treatment as well. Mix 3 tablespoons of neem oil to 4 liters of water, and spray onto affected plants every 7-14 days. Avoid spraying the plant's buds and flowers.

42. No More Leftovers: Apple Cider Vinegar Made from Peels and Cores

To make apple jam, the first thing we need to do is to peel and core the apples. That is a lot of waste, isn't it? Well, not exactly, if we can use them to make our apple cider vinegar, which is used in different cuisines. You only need three ingredients to make apple cider vinegar (ACV).

- 1.5kg of apple peels and core with seeds, or use the entire apple if you wish to. In fact, the overripe ones will do even better.
- 1.5 litres of non-chlorinated water.
- 120g of sugar for the peels and core or for each apple add a teaspoon of sugar.

This is how you can make ACV at home.

1. Take the peels and core or cut the entire apples into blocks, and place this in a large glass bowl or jar with at least a two-inch space left on top for the carbon dioxide gas to be released during fermentation.

2. Dissolve the sugar and water and pour the solution over the apple. Top it with more water if necessary. The apples must be submerged in the sugar water solution. Cover it with a clean cotton cloth so that it allows the carbon dioxide to escape. Change the cloth from time to time if it gets dirty.

3. Place the glass bowl on your counter at room temperature. Let this stand for about two weeks. Stir with a wooden spoon (no metal) every day. Every day you will notice a froth on top of the bowl. This is the fermentation in progress. At the end of the 2 weeks, the solids may start to settle at the bottom. Soon the mixture will have the aroma of an apple cider.

5. Strain the fermented mixture to remove all of the solids. Pour the liquid into another clean glass container. Cover the container with another fresh clean cotton cloth, secured with elastic bands, or put a light lid so that it continues to breathe. Place the jar in a dark area for another four weeks. This homemade ACV stays indefinitely.

43. Bee Forage Plants

A single bee colony can pollinate 300 million flowers each day. Cross-pollination helps the world's crops and wild plants to thrive. Honey bees are so important that farmers prefer to practise beekeeping alongside their farming so that they can provide pollination for their crops.

The bees visit flowering plants to obtain nectar, which along with pollen and saliva, is churned into sweet honey. Pollination is important. It leads to the production of the fruits we eat. and seeds that will create more plants.

Almost one of every three bites of food that we eat is pollinated by honeybees. Bees help to pollinate crops such as apples, almonds, broccoli, strawberries, cucumbers and other foods. Without bees, humans wouldn't have very much to eat. So we need to consciously protect bee colonies that are affected by climate change.

44. Terrarium: A Miniature Earth

A terrarium is a garden in a glass vessel. The glass represents the atmosphere, the garden and the Earth. It contains pebbles, charcoal, soil, moss and a variety of plants.

The plants inside the terrarium use the sunlight filtering through the glass to make food by photosynthesis, releasing oxygen in the process. This oxygen is used for respiration by the same plants, and they release carbon dioxide.

This rhythmic circular process continues as long as sunlight, oxygen, carbon dioxide and water are present in the glass vessel.

This rhythm will bring a constant supply of moisture and nutrients to the slow-growing plants, creating a closed self-sustaining ecosystem. Once established, a terrarium will need nothing from the outside world except for a little indirect sunlight.

This is an ideal way to enjoy a beautiful garden inside your living room that fully supports the concept of water conservation.

45. Terrarium Step by Step

If you have a green thumb and want to bring a garden into your living room, you can build your own.

You will require:

1. A glass container with a lid – representing the atmosphere, allowing sunlight to enter but preventing other substances such as gases and water from escaping.
2. Some white or coloured gravel / pebbles for water drainage.
3. Some charcoal to absorb impurities.
4. Garden soil articles like shells can be placed for an aesthetic look.
5. Put in some non-flowering plants—Crotons, small ferns, Dracaena, Pothos (money plant), Syngonium, Snake plant or Spider plant.
6. Create a water spray bottle.

Steps to making a terrarium:

1. Create a closed system: Use a container of any shape or size. The container must be of glass or any other clear substance through which light can pass.
2. Place a layer of pebbles or gravel to drain the excess water and to prevent plant roots from rotting. This forms the base of your terrarium.
3. Place a few pieces of charcoal on the drainage layer. The charcoal acts as a filter for impurities.
4. Add a layer of garden soil to anchor the plants and to provide nutrition.
5. Choose slow-growing plants and make sure not to overplant. Prune the plants, if needed, before placing them in the terrarium, and make sure they are free of insects and disease. Place the largest plants in the terrarium first. Then add the smaller plants.

a. Sprinkle water, if required.

6. Close the lid of the terrarium. Generally, the depth of the drainage material, charcoal, and soil should equal about one-third the height of the container.

46. Turn off That Camera

Just one hour of videoconferencing or streaming emits 150-1,000 grams of carbon dioxide. While every gallon of gasoline burned creates about 8,887 grams of CO_2.

Researchers have estimated that leaving our camera off during a web call can reduce these footprints by 96%. Streaming content in standard definition rather than in high definition (HD) also could bring an 86% reduction.

A lot of people have shifted to working remotely because of the COVID-19 pandemic. This means that most people who work from home do not drive to meetings as there are various webinar options to connect with people.

But we can do better than this. So, turning off the camera during virtual meetings, is a simple but extremely effective tip to go green with our internet use.

47. Protecting Mangrove Forests

Mangrove forests occupy the boundary between the land and the sea. They mainly grow in or next to areas between the high tide and the low tide. However, mangroves the world over are declining.

Dense mangroves act as a barrier against strong waves. They help to reduce their power before they hit the coastal areas and cause huge damage. By protecting the existing mangrove forests and allowing them to spread from their original habitats, we can reduce the effects of climate change.

48. DRAM

Several technologies have matured that allow people to recycle waste plastic directly by 3D-printing it into valuable products, at a very nominal cost. Instead of purchasing, people are using their own recycled plastic to make decorative items, gifts, home and garden products, accessories, shoes, toys, sporting goods and gadgets from millions of free designs. Every kind of plastic waste, from used packaging to broken products can be used. This approach is called Distributed Recycling and Additive Manufacturing, or DRAM for short. Research has shown this approach to recycling and manufacturing is not only better for the environment, but it is also highly profitable for individual users making their own products. Some people are even setting up their own low cost small and medium-sized businesses. Making one's own products from open-source designs saves money and the environment as well.

49. Garuda Saviours

Greater Adjutant Storks are one of the most threatened stork species in the world. It is classified as endangered on the International Union for Conservation of Nature's Red List of threatened species and listed under Schedule IV of the Indian Wildlife (Protection) Act, 1972.

To protect these endangered birds or "Garuda" (as the bird is called among the villagers of the riverine floodplains belt in Bhagalpur district of Bihar) is now a priority along with tending to their winter rabi crop.

Earlier, these birds were ignored as the local farmers were not aware of its importance. Mishra, a bird expert, first spotted Greater Adjutant Storks nesting and breeding in the riverine areas in Bhagalpur. He motivated different communities in these sleepy villages of Kadwa Diara to work for conservation. Initially suspicious, the villagers and fisherfolk of the region soon realised the importance of the Garuda. Crops are their lifeline and source of livelihood. They realised that these birds provide agrarian benefits by eating rats, snakes and insect pests.

A team of young Garuda Saviours have successfully convinced local villagers not to cut old trees and to plant saplings to increase the number of trees favoured by Greater Adjutant Storks.

50. Clover Plants in Your Garden

The diverse colours of clover flowers are beautiful. They are very useful as they attract beneficial insects for pollination and promote a healthy lawn. Clovers are nitrogen-fixing plants, which means they can trap the free nitrogen gas from the air, and change it into organic compounds. These organic compounds are used by plants. They also help to enrich and rejuvenate the soil.

Clover is easy and cost-effective to grow. Mix clover seeds with sand, sawdust, fine compost, or soil for even distribution and scatter it over the planting area. After sowing, water the planting site and keep the soil surface moist until the clover germinates.

Clover grows quickly, bringing unexpected beauty in a variety of colours, from pink and purple to deep crimson.

51. Clover Lawns in Your Garden

Intermixing clover with turf grasses makes lawns easier to manage. This is how it works:

- Clover lawns require little water and pesticide. When we intermix clover in our lawns, turf grasses benefit as clover fixes nitrogen and feeds the organic compound produced to the grasses. This reduces the need for adding fertilisers to improve soil health.
- The soil health also improves as the combination of tap roots and fibrous roots of the clover plant help to aerate the soil. It protects soil from wind and water erosion. A clove cover maintains soil moisture and suppresses weeds.

52. Other Advantages of Clover Plants

There is a popular saying that if you have eaten honey, you have eaten clover too. Clover is one of the honeybees' favourite foods. So, pollinators and other beneficial insects like ladybeetles, minute pirate bugs or flower bugs, lacewings, tiny parasitoid wasps, are attracted to clover for food – nectar and pollen. In return, these garden predators efficiently perform the job of biological pest controllers and feed on pests like aphids, whiteflies, scales, cabbage worms, and other garden pests. Hence, by planting clovers and other flowers to attract these natural predators, we take a big step towards managing pest problems in the garden in a natural way without polluting the environment with harmful chemicals.

Clovers are edible and have medicinal value. Clovers also have a long history of being considered as a powerful herb with medicinal properties to relieve pain and inflammation. They are high in antioxidants and popularly used as cleansing tea. Both white and red clover are also used as blood thinners.

Red clover is used in medicines that help prevent cancer, indigestion, high cholesterol, whooping cough, cough, asthma and bronchitis.

53. Wild Plants You Can Snack On

When you are hiking, camping, fishing or exploring the beautiful world outside, you will always come across wild plants. Some of these wild plants can be eaten as natural snacks. These natural snacks do not need to be wrapped in plastic or preserved, and hence these snacks are healthy and do not add to the pollution of the environment.

Blackberries are a universal favourite. These fruits can be easily recognised from their bunched fruits ranging from green and light pink to red and deep blackish-purple colours. They are sweet to slightly tart, succulent, soft and juicy fruits which are 100% safe to eat.

Clovers are found everywhere in the open area. They are easily spotted by their distinctive leaves. One can eat them raw. The pink and white blossoms taste better, but need to be taken in moderation.

54. More Snacks in the Wild

Amaranth is a weed that grows wild and all parts can be eaten. Its leaves are sweet to eat. Amaranth is considered a superfood as it is rich in proteins, gluten-free and cholesterol-lowering, low in carbohydrates and containing vitamins like A, C, E, K and B6 folate riboflavin. They also contain rich antioxidants which help to keep your body disease-free. They are enriched with calcium and magnesium. Being natural, they are environmentally safe as well.

Dandelion is commonly found in the wild as an edible weed. The entire plant is edible: roots, leaves and flowers. Young leaves taste better than the mature ones which have a bitter taste to them. The dandelion flower makes an excellent garnish for a salad. Roots can be boiled to make tea. It serves as herbal medicine and is used to treat loss of appetite, stomach related ailments, gallstones, muscle and joint aches and many other ailments.

55. Wild Snacking Continues

Chickweed is a low-growing plant with bright green, pointed oval leaves placed opposite each other. They have very distinct white small flowers which seem to be having ten petals but actually, they are five with incomplete splits. It is highly nutritious, containing vitamins, minerals and omega-6 fatty acid. Young leaves can be used in salads. However, if too much chickweed is eaten, it can cause diarrhoea, so must be taken in moderation.

56. Plantain (Jangli Isabgol/Asvagola)

This weed grows just about anywhere and is often found on the edges of gardens or driveways. It is considered one of the best healing herbs on the planet. It has a long history of being used to heal wounds, cure fever, and draw out toxins from stings and bites, including snakebites. All one needs to do is chew the leaves, take them out and put them over the bite area. You might come across mainly two types (extra space) of plantains; the ones with broad leaves and the narrow-leaved ones. Both are used for healing purposes, but the broadleaf plantain is preferred for its young, softer, edible leaves. However, seeds of both can be eaten right away.

57. ACV: A Health Wonder

Apple cider vinegar can be effectively used against many different kinds of pathogens because of its highly acidic nature. It is used to clean and disinfect wounds, treat nail fungus, lice, warts and ear infections.

Antimicrobial: This antimicrobial nature of ACV also makes it a great preservative for food, and studies have shown that it prevents the growth of microbes like E. coli in food.

Detox drink: In fact, taking the diluted 2 tablespoons of ACV (not more) in 250ml water a day can do wonders, as it works on acid reflux, relieves night leg cramps, removes bad breath, keeps the heart healthy and has weight loss benefits too.

58. ACV - A Beauty Armour

Apple cider vinegar is not just great for our health but also offers skin benefits.

Nobody wants acne, especially on the face. Apple cider vinegar works to control acne as our skin is naturally acidic and it helps to replenish the acidic layer of the skin. When our face is cleaned with ACV , it helps to ward off germs and kills bacteria. In this process, it removes the grease and dirt as its astringent properties increase blood flow to the face and tones the skin acting as an exfoliator to remove dead skin cells.

Mix half a cup of apple cider vinegar with 4 cups of water and apply the solution to the sunburnt skin. Or mix a cup of apple cider vinegar, 1/4 cup coconut oil and lavender essential oil into your bath water to soothe your skin.

59. Improve Soil Organically

A balanced combination of different elements is required for various plant processes and also to keep the soil healthy. There are several natural products that we use daily but of which we throw away the rest as waste. Yet on closer look, the so-called organic waste is packed with rich elements.

How do you like your eggs in the morning? When boiling eggs, the calcium leaches into the water, making it an excellent calcium feed for the plants when cooled. Enjoy the eggs in any way but don't throw away the shells. These are loaded with calcium, so, sprinkle the crushed dry eggshells around tomatoes, peppers, eggplants, and squash plants.

They also keep the snails and slugs away. If you add them to the compost bin, their lime content reduces the acidity of the compost. To top this, half eggshells can be used as an effective seedling bed for plants. Just poke a hole at the base for excess water drainage, fill them with soil and sow the seeds. After the seedlings have emerged and developed their first mature leaves, break off the bottom part of the eggshell and transplant the whole seedling shell with the soil into a larger pot or garden.

60. Power of Small Actions

In a crisis, we must protect the most vulnerable. Climate change and COVID-19 are two very different challenges, but they do have some key things in common. Both are global crises and strike with no respect to national boundaries, governments, and businesses. The individuals of global communities need to address the crises and take measures.

Around the world, by staying inside and taking their climate marches online, concerned citizens are raising their voices on an unprecedented scale, showing solidarity with the older members of society, who are more vulnerable to the virus. They are asking leaders to protect them from climate change.

A good education is one of the most valuable tools we have to fight climate change, because it provides children and young people with the skills and knowledge they need to create a better tomorrow. We can all play a part in sharing accurate facts around science, countering the misinformation that puts lives at risk.

61. Miracle Moringa

Moringa oleifera is a plant that has been praised for its health benefits for thousands of years. Scientific research on the moringa plant has concluded that it is extremely nutritional and medicinal. It is a fast-growing, drought-resistant tree often called the drumstick tree, horseradish tree or ben oil tree. Extracts of this plant help to take care of glowing skin and hair. Regular intake of this superfood helps to regulate high blood pressure, improves vision and might help a person's body absorb more iron, therefore increasing their red blood cell count. It is thought the plant extract is very helpful in treating and preventing anaemia and sickle cell disease. All in all, it is a wonder plant and considered a superfood.

62. Altered Biodegradability

While purchasing goods, we often come across some products which are given a preference because they have a label that reads 'BIODEGRADABLE'. So, we automatically presume them better and safer for the planet. Well, that depends!

Take a tree for instance. As long as it lives, it acts as a carbon sink by utilising the carbon dioxide and giving out oxygen. During its lifetime it keeps shedding leaves, branches, fruits and flowers that turn into manure, replenishing the soil. Eventually, when the tree dies naturally, it degrades, and slowly releases the stored-up carbon back into the atmosphere. But the whole scenario changes when the same tree is cut and turned into paper teacups by industries! Discarded paper teacups usually end up in landfills. Since they are processed with chemicals and lined with a thin film of plastic to make them waterproof the natural decomposition process of the wood pulp-turned-paper teacups gets altered.

63. Natural Bioindicators

Lichens are the greenish patches we find on trees and rocks. Lichens can be found all around the planet from freezing areas in the Antarctic to hot, tropical belts. Some can survive the harsh climatic changes for years. Lichens absorb atmospheric moisture to survive. If the air is contaminated with high levels of pollutants, then it becomes difficult for most lichens to survive. Hence, lichens are the ideal indicators of how polluted the air is around us. There are three main types of lichens found in nature:

Flat, leaf-like lettuce full of ridges and bumps are the Foliose Lichens.

Coral-like upright shrubby or bushy growth structures are the Fruticose Lichens.

The Crustose Lichens, as the name suggests, form a crust, pressed over any surface like rocks, boulders, soil, roofs, etc. They are found in many vibrant colours from grey, green to bright red-orange.

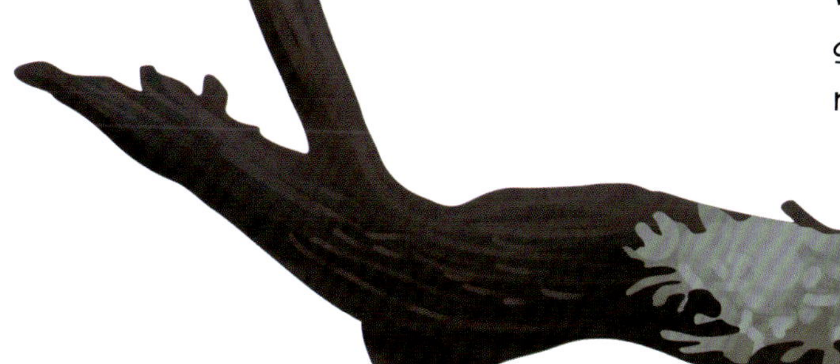

Where can lichens survive and not survive?

- In an area that is affected by a pollutant like sulphur dioxide, most likely the sensitive shrubby Fruticose Lichens will be absent.
- An area that is a bit more polluted will also have the leafy Foliose Lichens absent from there.
- But in areas that are heavily polluted not only by sulphur dioxide but also by oxides of other pollutants like nitrogen, there is a high chance of having a complete absence of lichens altogether on rocks and barks of trees.

64. Go Bananas with Soil

Banana skin is packed with potassium that strengthens stems and protects plants from disease. It also contains phosphorus which helps the plant to survive harsh winters. The potassium helps to speed up flowering and fruiting. Along with these, a banana peel also contains some additional minerals like calcium, manganese, sodium, magnesium, and sulphur. These these minerals help in plant functioning.

One of the benefits of fertilising with banana peels is that they break down quickly, thus making nutrients readily available to plants. They can be dried, crushed and sprinkled straight or buried deep in the soil. The peels can be chopped and submerged in water for a week to leach out the elements. Strain the peels out, and pour the solution on the soil to get the benefit of the nutrients without attracting pests.

65. Coffee, Me and Earthworms

Using coffee grounds as garden fertiliser is a great way to make use of something that would otherwise end up in a landfill. Coffee grounds can be easily composted and used as mulch. The caffeine in them repels slugs, snails and other pests and it is also a complete fertiliser.

Coffee has a large amount of nitrogen that can help the plants to grow faster. Along with that, it also has a fair amount of potassium and phosphorus. Hence, ground coffee offers all three essential ingredients: Nitrogen Phosphorus Potassium (NPK), required to make an ideal fertiliser for plant growth. The benefit of using coffee grounds as a fertiliser is that it also adds organic material to the soil, which improves drainage, water retention and aeration in the soil. The used coffee ground helps microorganisms to thrive which is beneficial to plant growth.

66. The Combo of Three

Coffee ground is full of our first nutrient: nitrogen!

Eggshells are full of our second nutrient: phosphorus!

Banana peels are full of our final nutrient: potassium!

Hence, remember, don't ever throw out your eggshells, banana peels, or used coffee grounds into the waste bins. Instead, use them to feed your plants. Just cut the banana peels into small pieces or dry them first and grind them. They can be used both ways, but if you want to store the mixture, the dried one will last longer. Same with the eggshells. Sun dry and crush them. Mix the two powders with the dried coffee ground all in equal proportion.

Through trial and error, you may learn the best way to use it. Simply sprinkle it on the topsoil or mix it with the potting soil. It can also be used by putting the mixture directly into the ground where your plants are growing. Simply dig a small hole far from the plant and spoon in your mixture, trying not to touch the plant root. Cover with soil and water as you normally would. Slowly, the nutrients will leach into the soil and fertilise it.

67. Poison – Good and Bad

The word 'POISON' evokes thoughts of evil. It is associated with a substance that is dangerous causing injury, illness or death. But for thousands of years, people have relied on poison for curative antidotes. Here are some natural poisons used as lifesaving drugs:

Foxgloves are known to be poisonous leaves. But they are used in lifesaving drugs that strengthen the heart.

The yew tree has a legendary connection to death. Its seeds, leaves and bark are highly toxic. But its reputation changed as a potential healer and preserver of life as it effectively inhibits the progress of some cancers.

Small doses of opium from poppy seeds, Mandrake's roots, Henbane's leaf and Hemlock's leaf, seed and roots are used as medicine to numb pain.

68. Saving the Environment

Our environment is facing many problems like global warming, ozone depletion, and climate change. Our landfills are getting bigger and multiplying in number all over. The air is getting more and more polluted. Clean drinking water resources are depleting and the land is getting choked.

Saying 'No' to air, water and land pollution are bigger issues, but they will all take shape and show effect eventually if we all start making small and simple changes in our daily lives. It will take time but is worth doing as we do not have another planet to move on to if this one becomes unliveable.

69. 'Sunglasses Effect'

Researchers found that the explosive volcanic eruptions of Katmai (Alaska, June 1912) and El Chichon (Mexico, April 1982) loaded the Northern Hemisphere with aerosols that led to the least active hurricane season on record in 1914 and 1983 respectively. Based on the satellite observation, geoengineers are working hard on developing a plan to pump sulfate into the atmosphere, as sulfates are known to block out some wavelengths of light. But there's one huge problem: Pumping that much sulfate into the atmosphere would perforate the protective ozone layer surrounding the Earth that is critical in protecting us from deadly radiation from the Sun. The geoengineers are already working on a mix of gases that mimic the shading property of sulfates. These artificial particles could be pumped into the atmosphere without shredding the ozone layer, and succeed in cooling down our oceans. Which in turn would reduce the number of Katrina-force hurricanes by half over the next 50 years.

70. Migration

Human migration due to changing climate happens primarily in poor communities and agriculture-dependent countries. It is prompted by changes in temperature, rainfall variability and rapid onset events such as storms, cyclones and floods. Experts believe that millions of people will be forced to flee their homes by the sudden onset of climate events like cyclones, floods and drought. They are referred to as climate migrants or climate refugees. A fresh approach to "climate change migration" is needed that takes human security as its starting point by reducing global temperature increases. This will in turn reduce the risk of population displacement due to climate change.

71. Indirect Way to Assess the Dissolved Oxygen Level

Nature has created many different types of natural indicators that can detect pollution in the environment. Let us read about some of the indirect ways of assessing oxygen levels in the water.

Caddisfly larvae thrive in high oxygen environments. Hence, the presence of a high amount of these larvae in water would be an indirect way to establish that the dissolved oxygen levels are 'high'.

The presence of dragonfly larvae suggest that the dissolved oxygen level in the water may be of a medium level.

A high abundance of blood worms or midge larvae, indicates that water has a very high level of pollution usually from sewage.

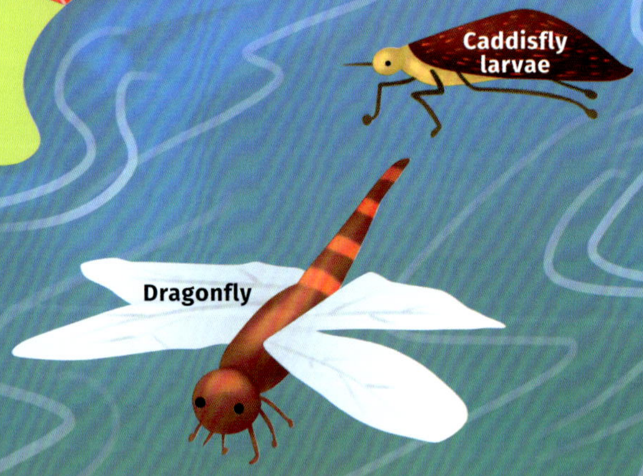

Caddisfly larvae

Dragonfly

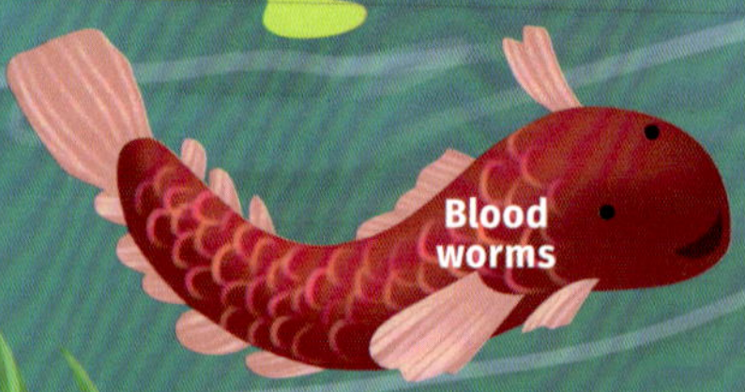

Blood worms

72. Simple Ways to Save the Environment: Natural Mosquito Repellents

The most effective way to control mosquitoes is to find and eliminate their breeding sites. Using safe and natural repellents will not only curtail the mosquito menace but will also safeguard our health. Chemical control of mosquitoes around the home may be accomplished with the use of repellents or sprays. Oil of citronella is a natural herb available in nature, which is a type of mosquito repellent. Oil of citronella is the active ingredient in many of the candles, torches, or coils which may be burned to produce smoke that repels mosquitoes. These are useful outdoors only under windless conditions. Other natural organic mosquito repellents like lemon eucalyptus oil, lavender oil, cinnamon oil, thyme oil, tea tree oil are equally effective.

73. Homemade Insecticides and Repellents

Organic pesticides can be made at home. Collect fresh neem leaves in a bowl. Peel and crush cloves. Mix the two. Add 2 liters of water and slow boil the mixture for about 20 minutes. Cool and then strain it. The colour changes to dull green. Transfer into an old plastic bottle. Spray the plants every alternate day, around 4-5 times. Repeat after a break of 10 days. Now spray organic neem garlic pesticide to kill the bugs easily.

Ingredients

Neem leaves:	One large bowl
Garlic cloves:	One large complete pod (about 50gms)
Water:	2 liters

74. Get Rid of White Mealybugs Using Homemade Pesticides

Mealybug is a plant-sucking bug. The bugs are usually covered with a white or grey mealy wax, which prevents pesticides from penetrating through the layer to kill them. So, first, this sticky layer needs to be removed, before the pesticide attacks the bugs. This is tricky, but the solution lies in the use of a simple homemade wax-removing solution called ethyl alcohol which can be easily made by using leftover rice and water.

Take a small, old plastic bottle (about 250ml). Add 5-6 spoons of leftover cooked rice. Top it with 100ml of water in an approximately 1:4 ratio of rice and water. Cap it, shake it and leave it for 10 days to ferment into ethyl alcohol. Transfer the solution into a spray bottle. Spray it over the white waxy coating and you will be able to scrape away the waxy layer as it dissolves with ethyl alcohol.

75. Garlic-Neem Oil Spray

Neem oil is made from the kernels of neem trees and has traditionally been used to treat anything from head lice to Malaria. It is an effective repellent and insecticide for hundreds of chewing and sucking insects that destroy the garden. But at the same time it is non-toxic to the useful bees. It also fights fungi, mildew and rust. Therefore, it is ideal to choose neem oil over the harmful toxic chemical insecticides available in the market.

Garlic, on the other hand, has been used for centuries as a natural healing medicine and a strong pesticide, known for its antibacterial, antiviral, and anti-fungal properties. This spray can be made at home.

Soak 100 g of finely minced garlic cloves in 2 teaspoons (tsp) of neem oil for at least 24 hours. Slowly add 1 liter of warm water with 1 teaspoon of oil soap mixed into it. Strain and store in a glass jar. To spray, use 1 litre of water with 2 tablespoons of the mixture. Use neem - garlic spray on affected plants 1-2 times per week until the infestation has gone. This is a cleaner and safer way to get rid of harmful bugs without causing any damage to the environment.

Ingredients

Garlic: Minced 100 grams

Neem oil: 2 teaspoons

76. Baking Soda Wonders

Baking soda is power-packed and has been used for thousands of years as a cleaning product for both our homes and our bodies. It is cheap and easily available in the market.

Here are some of the ways baking soda can be used in our daily lives.

Before	What to do?	After
	Soak combs and brushes in a mug of water with 1 teaspoon baking soda dissolved in it, for a few hours. Scrub and clean. The same process can be repeated with pots and pans.	
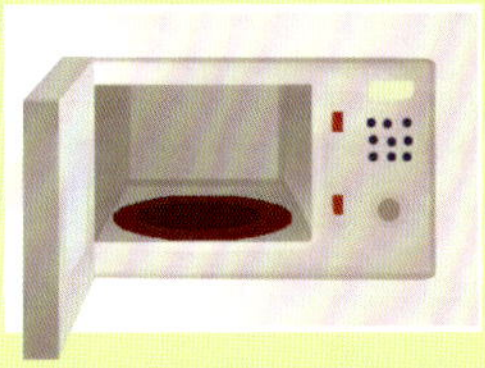	Sprinkle baking soda generously on the gas oven or microwave oven or tiles and scrub the surface thoroughly with an old wet towel. Remember not to use paper towels as that is a waste and a huge load on the environment.	
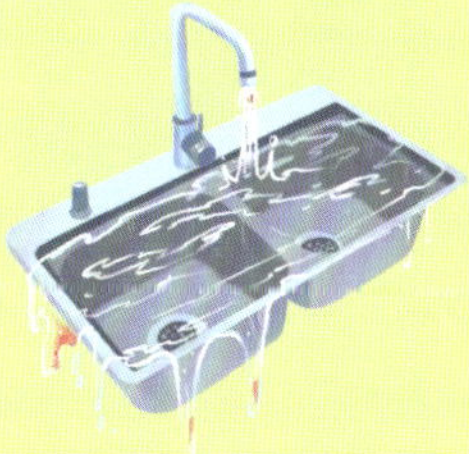	For blocked kitchen sinks, add baking soda generously. Pour vinegar over it and then hot water to open the block.	
	Sprinkling baking soda on wooden chopping boards and scrubbing and rinsing it under running water is an excellent non-toxic way to clean the board and remove odour too.	
	Baking soda absorbs odours from the rooms and helps to get rid of bad smells. To further deodorise household items, sprinkle baking soda over odour sources like carpets, furniture, mattresses. Place a small cup with a few spoons of baking soda powder in cupboards and refrigerators to remove odours.	

77. Get into the CITRUS Habit

It is common knowledge that citrus fruits are rich in Vitamin C. We usually eat the fruit and throw away the peel. What a waste! Get into the habit of using citrus oil which can be easily prepared at home It is an excellent repellent for common house and garden insects like mosquitoes, aphids, fleas, mites, houseflies, fruit flies and many other insect-pests. Spraying citrus oil mixed in soapy water will do the trick. Besides being an effective organic insecticide for plants, it can be safely applied to the skin to ward off insects like mosquitoes.

Collect citrus peels like lemon, orange, lime and others. You can make citrus oil at home. Grate, chop or crush 1/4th cup of the peel which is rich in minerals and essential oil. To this, add a cup of oil like almond, olive, soybean, sesame, canola or neem oil. Let it sit for some time in a dark cool place till the essence of the citrus infuses into the oil. Strain the oil, which can be kept in a glass bottle for months.

78. Cleaner, Safer Citrus Vinegar

There is more we can do with the citrus peels. We can make citrus vinegar, which is an excellent agent for cutting through grease and disinfecting. It can be easily made at home from citrus peels after squeezing out the juice from the fruit. Just put the peels in a glass jar and top it with vinegar. Let the peels sit in the vinegar for about a month to help dissipate the smell of vinegar and turn it into more of a citrus type of smell. This will allow all the essential oil to leach into the vinegar before it is ready for use. Once done, strain and store the liquid in an empty container while composting the peels.

Use 2-3 tbsp of citrus vinegar with 2-3 tsp of liquid soap. Dilute in 1 litre of water and use for any household cleaning of dishes, kitchen sinks, toilets, washing clothes or even as an air freshener. Using this solution will not pollute our water system.

79. Soap vs. Detergent— Your Choice!

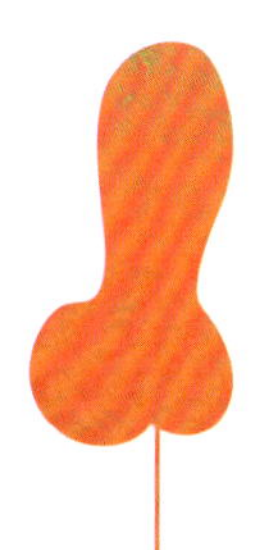

Soap and detergent have been used interchangeably for years, when in fact, they are quite different from each other. Let's find out more about their differences. Which one would you prefer to wash with? After all, what you need is something to cut grease, remove stains and allow you to live a non-toxic life.

SOAP	DETERGENT
Components used to make soap are fats, oil and water.	Detergent is a synthetically produced agent. This kind of substance tends to reduce the surface tension of a liquid in which it is dissolved.
Made from organic chemicals and is cheaper.	Made from inorganic chemicals and is comparatively costlier.
Soap is biodegradable and does not contain toxic chemicals that pollute rivers and streams. Some environmental impacts will be there but comparatively, it is eco-friendlier.	With many inorganic chemicals, it contaminates our water, thus affecting aquatic organisms. Detergents often cause allergies to the skin, as well.
Soaps are made of fat and alkali and do not dry the skin too much.	If it touches our skin it causes an imbalance in pH levels. Skin or clothes absorb natural oils causing dryness and damage to our skin.
Soaps are not as effective in washing a large number of clothes.	Detergents are much more powerful than soap, and it takes a small quantity to wash large volumes of clothing.
Soaps don't produce lather which can be a problem in cleaning clothes.	Detergents are effective in all types of water.
More water is required to remove soap.	Detergent can be washed off easily with a lesser amount of water.

80. Jewels of Nature

Have you ever noticed that nature provides plenty of jewels around you? All you need to do is develop an eye for it, appreciate it and preserve it in your memory or your phone gallery, which is easily available to you.

Hundreds and thousands of diamonds are found on the spider web formed by the monsoon dew.

Jewel bugs with metallic black-spotted red rubies embedded with corals can be seen crawling on leaves.

81. Nature Provides a Helping Hand

The leaves and stems of stinging nettle plants are covered with stinging hair. If by mistake, your skin touches or scrapes it, you will immediately feel as if you've been stung by a horde of angry ants or bees. It irritates and burns the skin causing immense pain. Dock leaves can bring instant relief to the painful sting. You can take a few leaves and rub them vigorously between your palms to release moist sap from the leaves. Then apply it to the affected area. This helps to immediately soothe the irritated skin and cool it down.

82. Turning Sand to Soil

Soil is composed of several minerals in combination with sand, silt and clay along with organic matter, air, and water.

Try growing plants in sand. It is difficult because water runs out of sand quickly and it can be hard for sand to retain the nutrients that plants need to grow. If a handful of soil is squeezed, and the texture feels gritty and it falls apart when you open your palm, then it is sandy soil which is primarily sand, made from small pieces of eroded rocks.

Sandy soil can easily be turned into normal soil just by increasing its ability to retain water and also by increasing the nutrients in the soil. We can add clay and silt to hold water in the soil. The combination of minerals and organic matter, aerates the soil, helps to improve its ability to hold onto water and add the nutrient value required to grow plants.

83. Brew Wood Ash Tea

Just like tea, wood ash tea can also be brewed, but it is not for drinking. It can correct the potassium deficiency in plants. Brown spots on the leaves, curling leaf tips, yellowing between leaf veins, slower plant growth and reduced crop yield means there is potassium deficiency.

To make the wood ash tea for the garden, take a large drum and add approximately 150 liters of water. Then, dip an old pillow bag filled with around 2 kilos of wood ash, with its top tied like a teabag. Allow the nutrients from the ash to soak and infuse into the water for several days. Once the ash tea has brewed, pour a cup of this tea weekly around the affected plants. After a few weeks, you will see the change as the plants absorb the potassium from the tea and become healthy.

84. STOP! Don't Throw Away Wood Ash

Wood ash, which is the residue after a pile of wood blocks burns, is rich in many minerals, mainly calcium, phosphorus, magnesium and potassium. It also contains small amounts of manganese, boron, copper, molybdenum, iron, sodium and zinc. It contains five times more nutrients than softwood if the ash is from hardwood.

Traditionally, it has been used by farmers to reduce acidity in the soil and replenish the nutrients in it. It is good for plants that require more potassium like tomatoes, broccoli, cabbage, beans, beets, asparagus, root vegetables. These vegetables grow better in neutral to slightly alkaline soil. Wood ash helps to get rid of weeds and creepy crawlies like slugs, snails and other pests like aphids and whiteflies that eat the flower beds. It also reduces the problem of algae in fish ponds without using any harmful chemicals. The soil should be properly raked and then sprinkled with a very thin layer of wood ash and then watered thoroughly.

Storage Tips:

- Store wood ash in an airtight container away from moisture.
- Protect seeds from fungus while preserving and storing. Mix the seeds with wood ash powder and seal them for storage. You can also use moisture-absorbing materials like charcoal powder or small pieces of newspaper.

85. Use Wood Ash Wisely

Wood ash is derived from burning wood which is a plant material, and it contains many essential nutrients required for plant growth. The carbonates and oxides in the ash can raise the pH and help neutralise acidic soils. But some precautions need to be taken before using wood ash.

- Do not use wood ash if your soil pH is alkaline. Do a pH test with a simple pH testing gadget available in the market before using wood ash.
- Wood ash is not good for acid-loving plants, such as berries like raspberries, strawberries, blueberries along with roses, rhododendrons, fruit trees, potatoes, parsley.
- Direct application of wood ash on new plant seedlings during germination can burn the plant as it contains too much salt.
- Wood ash is not recommended in areas used for growing potatoes. Though potassium is welcome, it increases alkalinity and encourages fungus and potato scab.
- Do not mix and apply wood ash with nitrogen fertilisers like urea as they emit ammonia gas when in contact with a high pH substance like wood ash.
- Use eye protection goggles and mask while handling fine particles of wood ash powder.

86. MethaneSAT

A SpaceX rocket will launch the new satellite MethaneSAT, to track the amount of methane in Earth's atmosphere in 2022.

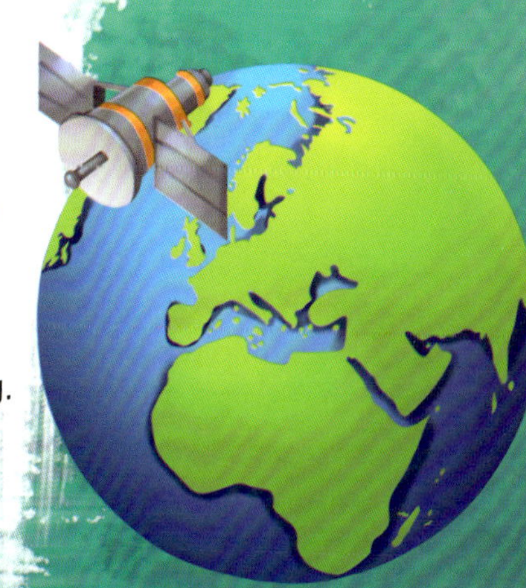

It is designed to do what no other satellite can do. It can detect and measure almost all human-caused methane emissions almost anywhere on the globe, across large regions while also measuring individual sites.

Reducing methane emissions from the oil and gas industry is the fastest, most cost-effective way to slow the rate of global warming. MethaneSAT is designed to create that transparency and ensure that companies and governments do not miss the opportunity and help combat climate change around the world.

87. Eco-friendly De-icers

Under sub-zero conditions in places where modern-day facilities are not accessible, people still depend upon the use of good old firewood to pass through the severe snow-covered winter months.

Eco-friendly home solutions like sand, gravel, wood chips, and sawdust have always been traditionally used. These provide traction due to their gritty texture but do not melt the ice. But, thawing leaves quite a messy clean-up task to be done later.

Ashes left after burning all night in the fireplace are very effective at melting ice on the pavements. They are good de-icers as they help to stop ice from forming, so that people can walk without slipping and getting injured. Wood ash contains potash – potassium salts – which will help de-ice and melt snow in moderate conditions. The best part is it's free and costs nothing. It does not cause harm to plants and animals when used because it is a natural product of the plant itself.

88. Don't Ignore the Peels

We throw away the peels of fruits and vegetables. Well, contrary to what you might think is WASTE, actually quite a few of them are brimming with flavour, and are packed with edible nutrients. So now think about it, when we throw these peels, we throw out FOOD. It doesn't make sense to throw out potato, orange or even apple peels when we can do so much with them. Your grandparents might have eaten tasty chips made from these. Here are some simple things we can do with peels to reduce waste. Wash the peels thoroughly before you proceed.

1. Ginger peel: Sun-dry or oven-dry the peels, grind them to a fine powder and store them for further use in tea, broths or stocks, and even curries.
2. Potato peel: New potatoes can be cooked with their skin on. They are yummy! The older ones have a thicker peel, so soak them in water for a while, drain, sprinkle with seasonings and brush with oil, and then air fry or bake in an oven till they turn crisp. Easy to make tasty snacks with your favourite dips for a party.
   The same can be done with sweet potatoes and carrots.

89. Recognise the Value of Peels

Browse the internet and find out what else you can do with the peels before you trash them. Also, maybe you can find out an old grandmother's recipe using peels and try your hand at it.

1. Lime, lemon and orange peel: Who can resist the sweet, tangy aroma of these brightly coloured citrus fruits? Sun-dry or oven-dry these peels and then grind them into a fine powder. The smell is unbeatably fresh and therapeutic. Store the powder in an airtight container and use it to flavour cakes and desserts. This powder can be added to teas for a dash of citrus flavour.
2. Apple: While it's best to have apples with the skin itself, a lot of people do peel this fruit. Apple crispies are delicious, crunchy and mildly sweet. You can grind them to make apple flavoured tea or add more sugar to make apple jam or ACV.
3. Watermelon peel: The mildly sweet watermelon can be added to sweet candy, spicy curry, pickle, salsa dip or jam.

90. Repurposing: Plastic Bottles

Finding empty plastic bottles of all kinds in a home is a very common feature. Over 100 million used plastic bottles are discarded every day, with approximately 80 per cent of them simply becoming non-biodegradable harmful litter mainly for marine life.

Repurposing plastic bottles is an excellent habit to get into if we want to do our share to help save the environment. They are great for sharing innovative ideas to create decors and functional bottle crafts.

91. Repurpose: Plastic Bottles as Life Savers

Plastic bottle boats are not only lightweight but can be effective in carrying out rescue operations during floods.
Floats and waterproof slippers too can be made out of plastic bottles and used when travelling in waterbodies.
Low-cost sustainable and durable houses can be built with discarded plastic bottle walls. These plastic walls can provide excellent insulation from extreme heat as well as cold.
Flattened bottle roofs are not only cheap and durable but are also waterproof.
Footpaths made using bottle caps are creative, colourful and durable.

92. Repurposed Furniture

Repurposing means taking an item and changing its use. Repurposing and reusing items has many benefits. It is a great way to save money. It reduces the load on landfills. It also reduces the amount of material used to make new items. This is because the wood from old wooden furniture gets seasoned over the years, increasing its strength and stability. Repurposed furniture can be used to make tables, chairs, cupboards and other wooden items.

93. Kitchen Scrub

We can make a difference if we can replace the plastic non-biodegradable kitchen sponge scrub, which we use for only a few weeks before throwing it away. Each home can reduce the load on the landfill if we can replace the plastic scrub with three other equally effective things.

1. Old cotton towels or T-shirts can be cut into a convenient size for wiping. They can be easily tossed into the washing machine or hand washed, when dirty, and reused again and again.
2. A plant-based dish scrubber works more effectively and lasts longer too. When worn out, it can be easily recycled and composted.

3. For tough food stains, nothing can beat the natural coconut husk scrubs which are biodegradable and can be used as a fibre base for compost pits.

We don't need these synthetic kitchen sponges as they will never biodegrade in the landfills and will keep adding to the pollution. It would be better to switch back to the good old method of using washable, compostable scrubs.

94. Power of Rooftop Garden

Planting rooftop gardens in large urban spaces and utilising these unused wasted spaces more productively is the practical way to fight against climate change.

Rooftop gardens create a buffer and prevent heat from entering the building, This, in turn, reduces energy consumption as they provide added insulation in the colder months and prevent excessive heat absorption in the summer. Thus, rooftop gardens help to reduce building heating and cooling costs. Growing a green roof can extend its life by blocking out ultraviolet light.

Green roofs can be transformed into natural habitats for biodiversity. They serve as a refuge for creatures that struggle for survival by providing them with a safe habitat. Ground-nesting birds can safely use green roofs for nesting and raising their young, while migratory species use them as stopover shelters.

Rooftop gardens can also be used to produce healthy, nutritive, organic and fresh food for all seasons.

95. Mud House Built from Excess Mud from Land

Kerala-based Basheer Kalakkal's mud house is as spacious as a modern-day house. It is built over 1,090 sq ft, with three bedrooms with attached bathrooms, a kitchen, a work area, a hall, and an outdoor seating area. His love for the environment took him down this path to build his mud house surrounded by fruit trees.

All the mud used for construction was taken from the land itself. As the land was on a slant, he had to level it using an earth mover. The excess mud was collected and used for building his house. Fine mud was taken by removing the thicker mud by hand. Powder soil was used in the correct proportion to set up the mud house. He used normal tiles for the floors and fired-clay tiles for the roof.

Basheer follows Zero Budget Natural Farming (ZBNF), which helps plants grow naturally without the use of pesticides or fertilisers. He takes up contracts from people who wish to have this system in their homes or on their lands.

96. Packaged Food

Processed and packaged foods can be fast and convenient options for meals and snacks, but they are not always the healthiest choices. They are packed with unhealthy ingredients, which have negative effects if consumed regularly. Read the nutritional facts on the back of these food packets before you put them in your cart.

Ingredients	Limit consumption	if taken is excess
Sodium	2,300 milligrams/ day	High blood pressure Diabetes Kidney disease
Sugar	Women should consume no more than 100 calories from added sugars per day. Men should consume no more than 155 calories per day (1 gram of sugar = 4 calories).	Diabetes High cholesterol Heart disease Obesity Tooth decay
Additives make it more appealing as well as improve the flavour, shelf life, safety or nutritional quality of packaged food.	Chemicals like: olestra, aspartame, artificial colours and flavours, monosodium glutamate, saccharin, sodium nitrate, sulphites, cyclamate, caffeine, BHA, BHT and acesulfame-potassium should be avoided. The longer the list, the less healthier it is!	Some people may have adverse reactions to certain additives, as some are carcinogenic in nature. After all, they are all chemicals and not at all natural.

97. Farmers' Market

The farmers' market is becoming a popular concept in several towns and cities. In these markets, you can directly buy your food from the farmers of your choice. The idea is to get seasonal and locally grown food easily. These markets provide benefits for growers, consumers and the community.

Farmers' markets need less transportation, less handling, less refrigeration and less time in storage. Cutting out these steps reduces the carbon footprint.

The consumers are happy to get locally grown, fresh, and healthy food straight from the farm. Since the source is known to them, there is a smaller chance of the produce being contaminated with harmful pesticides. These markets promote safer, healthy food.

These markets also help to maintain farmlands and green open spaces in the community.

98. Textile Facts

Billions of articles of clothing are produced and sold around the world yearly. This, in turn, means billions of used articles of clothing are thrown away to make room for new ones every year. This a waste of valuable resources. Here are some interesting facts about textiles:

1. It takes more than 2500 litres of water to make a cotton shirt. That is equivalent to 900 days of drinking water for one.
2. This huge amount of textile waste produces toxic greenhouse gases. These gases are exceedingly harmful. They are emitted into the atmosphere, causing global warming.
3. Clothes can take up to 40 years to decompose, particularly synthetic clothing where it may take hundreds of years.
5. Textiles can be repurposed into many items.
6. When you donate clothing to charities, it's not uncommon for the clothing to be sold.

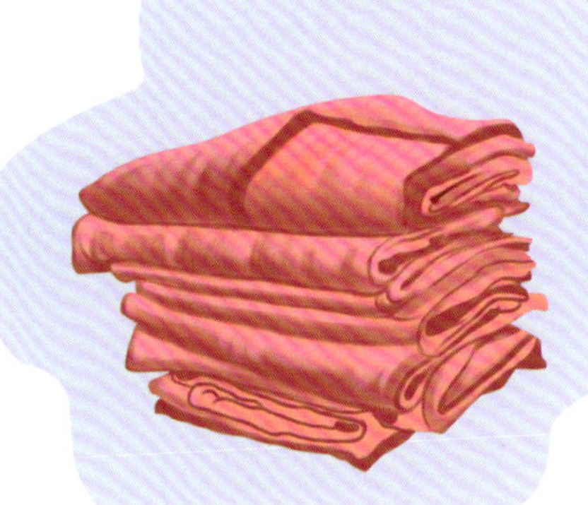

99. Red, a Sign of Warning

Giving up the consumption of red meat can help the environment in a big way. Let us read more about the effects of red meat production.

- The production, processing and distribution of meat require huge amounts of pesticides, fertilisers, fuel, food and water. The production process also releases greenhouse gases, and a range of toxic chemicals into air and water.
- 15% of all emissions are due to agriculture, half of which are from livestock, causing significant global warming.
- 70% of the deforestation of the Amazon jungle is done to provide land for cattle ranches.
- Red meat production uses more land and freshwater, and generates more greenhouse gas emissions per unit of protein, than any other commonly consumed food.

100. Waste not, Want Not

Globally, farmers work very hard to produce the food that we eat. After going through a long journey of using natural resources, food goes through processing in the kitchen before it comes to our dining table as the tasty and nourishing produce essential for life. Yet we throw away loads of it without blinking an eye.

When WE WASTE FOOD, we waste other things too.

- We waste precious water.
- We waste farming land.
- We waste money.
- We waste fuel.
- We waste energy.
- We contribute to global warming.

We can change this. Starting at home, each one of us can stop wasting food. This is possible if we collectively make a conscious decision to fight hunger, malnutrition, and take care of our planet.

101. Underground Park Tank

The impact of climate change is seen in many cities of the world in the form of:

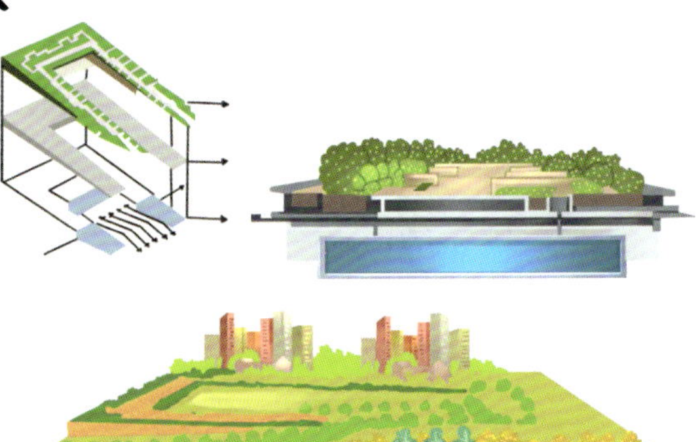

- Powerful storms.
- Extreme rainfall— too much and too quickly.
- Depletion of water due to the rise in temperature.
- Rising sea levels and sinking cities.
- More and more people moving to cities, more and more land getting paved.

To counter this, Bangkok has built an innovative park that controls floods in the city. The excess rainwater flows into a massive underground tank as big as a football field, built underneath the park. This tank has the capacity to hold 3.8 million liters of rainwater, good enough to water the entire park for some time. The park helps to retain and redirect floodwater that would otherwise flow into city streets.

As floods in cities are becoming a norm, we can take a few lessons from this innovation.

102. Palm Oil Plantation at the Cost of Rainforest... not a Good Idea!

Deforestation will only lead to depletion and loss of biodiversity. This has long-term health effects and a severe impact on global warming. Palm oil plantations are one such example.

Palm oil grows well in hot, humid climates. This leads to the clearing of rainforests by using slash-and-burn agriculture, which is the cruellest and quickest way to clear the land. It is estimated that millions of hectares of rainforest have already been lost to make way for palm oil plantations. But at what cost?

- It has had a hugely damaging effect on the animals and humans dependent on forests.
- It has endangered the Orangutans, who have lost 80% of their natural habitats.
- Only a few hundred Sumatran tigers are left in the wild.
- Indigenous people who depend on the forests for livelihood have had to give up and move out as they were unable to follow their way of life.
- People had to give up their land for palm oil plantations.

103. Palm Oil Impact

Environmental and social impacts of palm oil production are responsible for environmental damage, including an increase in global greenhouse gas emissions due to the clearing of large areas of rainforest for palm oil.

Consuming palm oil products is bad for us. They have unhealthy unsaturated fat and are high in calories, leading to heart disease, obesity, diabetes and other health issues. Supermarkets are full of food products that have palm oil, often listed as vegetable oil, to trick the customer. Starting from candies to bakery products and ice-creams to chips, all these foods have palm oil. Beauty products like lipsticks, shampoo, and soap have palm oil in them. Read the label next time before buying your favourite product. Be more conscious and cautious of the food you put in your mouth. Better still, give up junk food when you have safer, cheaper and healthier alternatives available to you.

104. Discover the Use of By-products

A by-product is the result of another action, often unforeseen or unintended. Researchers are constantly working to find solutions to handle every product and its by-products produced naturally or manufactured.

Let's take dairy farming for example. Cows are bred in dairies to produce milk that is sold in the market. The faeces and urine of the cow are the by-products created here during the process. These are organic materials, which farmers can use. Farmers can also commercially sell these by-products as manure, a fertiliser that can be used in home gardens, other farms or even companies depending upon how much by-product is generated.

105. STOP and SAVE

You can STOP or at least help reduce the amount of deforestation. Conserve the use of natural resources such as wood, oil and gas, electricity, and water.

Here are some things you can do to help:

- Always use both sides of the paper for writing, drawing, photocopying, and printing.
- Separate at source and recycle paper, cans, glass, and plastic.
- Try and read newspapers online.
- Go for recycled paper products: notebook paper, books, etc.
- Paper towels lead to the felling of trees, so use old washable towels instead. If you must, use recycled paper towels.
- Bidet or a hand-held bidet shower is cleaner and more hygienic than toilet paper. If you must go for toilet paper, use the one made from recycled paper.
- Use pencils until they are stubs.
- Buy furniture and wood that are certified as legally cut-down. Better still, repurpose old furniture.
- Eat organic fruits and vegetables, where no poisonous chemicals like insecticides or pesticides are sprayed on the food.
- Encourage your parents, relatives, and friends to get the PUC (Pollution Under Control) certificate for their vehicles.
- Whenever possible, walk, bike, carpool or use public transport.
- Save electricity at all times. Do not forget to switch off from the mains, as plugged-in appliances on standby mode also waste electricity.
- Save water at all times. Fix leaking taps.
- While washing your hands and brushing your teeth, turn off the water. You will save gallons of water.
- When doing the dishes, turn off the water while washing with soap. Rinse quickly after washing.
- Do not use a hosepipe to wash a car. Instead, reuse soapy water from washing machines. Save precious water at all times.

106. By-products of Almonds

Just a handful of almonds every day helps to lead a healthy life. Almonds contain one-eighth of our daily protein needs, along with vitamins, minerals, and fibres. Almonds are processed in a huller machine to separate the almond meat from the hull and shell. The hulls, shells and hash are the by-products that can be sold commercially in the market.

The table below will give the details.

Almond by-product	Description	Usage
Almond Hull	This is the outermost green covering layer of the almond while unplucked. When the hull splits, the almonds are ready to be harvested.	A cheaper and nutritious fibre source for livestock feed. Dairy milk production increases when almond hulls are part of a balanced feed.
Almond Shell	Almond shells are the hard layer between the hull and the almond meat. This is a protective layer that keeps pests and diseases away.	Broken and ground-up shells are also used as gardening mulch, landscape materials, bedding products for the dairy or poultry industry and mineral mix for livestock feed. It can be used as a fuel source, glue filler for laminate boards and other kinds of boards.
Almond Hash	These are pieces of almond meat produced during the shelling process, usually accompanied with small pieces of almond hull and shell.	This by-product can be used for livestock feed, pressed for almond oil and used as bird seeds.

107. Power of Cow Dung: Turn a Turbine

You may have heard about making manure from cow dung. How about turning it into electricity? Here are some things which can be done on dairy farms.

Flatten the cow dung into flat patties and sun-dry them till they dehydrate to become hard and dry.
Dry patties on fire burn easily to produce heat, causing water to heat up and boil to produce steam. • In winters, the heat generated can keep your house warm. • The heat can be used to dehydrate or dry agricultural produce.
The steam produced from boiling water can be used to turn a turbine connected to a generator to produce electricity.

108. Power of Cow Dung: Biogas

You can build a mini biogas plant for your house. The basic principles remain the same.

1. A slurry can be made of cow dung by mixing it with an equal part of water. A catalyst such as food compost matter will hasten the decomposition process.
2. The slurry is placed in a digester machine, which is an airtight container that will not allow the biogas, which is methane, to escape. Methane is produced when the dung and water decompose at 37 °C temperature.
3. Over 5-6 days, the microbes in the dung, in the absence of air and in a warm surrounding, get activated and eat the nutrients present in the slurry and produce methane biogas. Once there's enough methane gas in the machine, it is released from the digester to be used.
4. Most digester machines holding manure for biogas production are specially made so that they are easily hooked up with a pipe to a gas stove in the kitchen, used for cooking or to an ignition engine or can be used as a generator to produce electricity.
5. The by-products of biogas plants are the remaining liquids and solids that are separated in the digester to be reused.

The liquids are reused to make more slurry.

The solids are reused in bedding or fertiliser for livestock.

109. Reduce 'FOODPRINT'

Here are things you can do to reduce your 'FOODPRINT':

1. Eat vegetarian food. By now you know that fruits and vegetables produce fewer greenhouse gases than non-vegetarian food.
2. Eat home-cooked food. This will save you time, money and fuel.
3. Cook, serve and eat right away. Your 'foodprint' goes down when you do not reheat.
4. Eat organic food. Not only health-wise but environmentally also, it is better, sustainable and safe for all.
5. Save water. Water is the most precious natural commodity, and at every step of the food production, we need to use it cautiously as well as wisely.
6. Shop wisely. Before putting a food product in your cart, THINK! Do you need it? Is there a greener alternative?
7. Shop local, shop fresh. This way your carbon footprint comes down drastically as you are saving on transportation and refrigeration.
8. Grow your food. Anybody can do it, any place, anywhere. Use your imagination and reduce your 'foodprint'.
9. Reduce. Reuse. Recycle. These are the fantastic "Rs" and the list goes on. Be alert and give it a TRY every time.

SHOP LOCAL

PAPER

110. Weakening Our Future Health

Most human disease-causing pathogens came from animals. Covid-19 has put the spotlight on the origins of diseases. Buying, selling, and slaughtering wild animals for food is one way an animal-borne disease may infect people. Viruses can spread more easily if animals in markets are sick or kept in dirty, cramped conditions, such as in overcrowded cages. When wild animals are under stress, viral pathogens can intermingle, swap bits of their genetic code, and perhaps mutate in ways that increase the chance of diseases spreading from wildlife to humans. This act of ours not only threatens the human race but also biodiversity.

In order to halt this biodiversity loss, concerted action by multiple players is needed on climate change, land degradation, pollution and damage to the environment. Pharma and the traditional medicine industry should be spearheading this effort.

111. Carbon Footprint: Paper Tree

When you go to your school or visit your family or friends you take different means of transportation which runs on petrol, diesel or even gas. The carbon footprint is the total amount of carbon dioxide and methane gas released into the atmosphere by burning fuel and consuming energy. The more fuel we use, the bigger our carbon footprint.

If we are careful, we can save energy and reduce our footprint.

Let's take paper for example. We know it comes from trees. But do you know how many units of energy are used to make paper from a tree, that adds to carbon emissions?

Check it out and calculate.

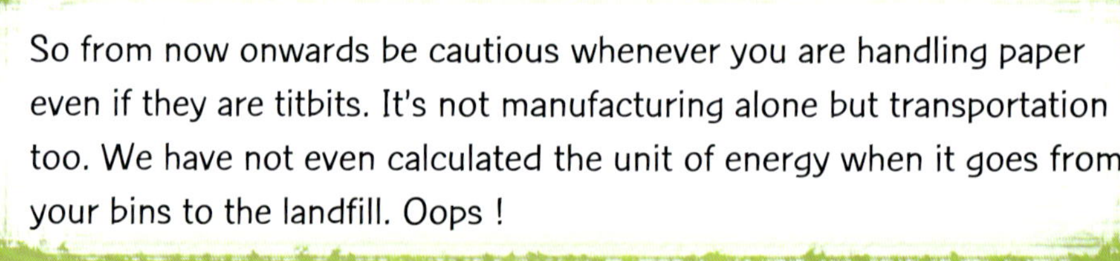

So from now onwards be cautious whenever you are handling paper even if they are titbits. It's not manufacturing alone but transportation too. We have not even calculated the unit of energy when it goes from your bins to the landfill. Oops !

112. Adding the Footprints

Driving a car will leave a carbon footprint. Is that the only carbon the engine releases?

Let's look into this process more deeply.

The car's fuel tank is filled in a local fuel station. Where does the fuel in the station come from? Consider the carbon that is emitted just to get that fuel into the car.

- Carbon is emitted for the energy needed to extract the oil from underground.
- Carbon is emitted while transporting the oil extracted to the refineries.
- Carbon is also emitted while oil is refined through various processes to get the fuel.
- Carbon is emitted to make the final destination and deliver the fuel to the local fuel station where we fill up the car fuel tanks.
- With the carbon emitted to manufacture the car in the first place, the footprint will be huge!

The bottom line is everything we use, leaves carbon footprints, some big, some small. It is up to us to reduce our footprint because our actions and choices will leave a personal mark on this planet that will stay long after we are gone.

113. Coffee in 'COFFEE' Cups

Can you imagine drinking coffee in a "coffee" cup? No, you didn't get it right, I mean, the cup is made of COFFEE— "leftover ground coffee" to be precise, which otherwise gets thrown into a bin.

It would be a positive step if the entire world joins hands to eliminate all kinds of disposable things that we usually use and replaces them with reusable, recyclable and biodegradable things instead! A start-up company, Kaffeeform, has introduced long-lasting reusable cups made from used coffee ground and is doing this to reduce the use of disposable coffee cups that we get in cafes.

They are drying out the leftover coffee, which is sourced from different coffee shops, mixing it with natural glues and wood particles, to be remoulded into sustainable coffee cups. The best part is that these cups are reusable as they are dishwasher-friendly and can last for years. Once the cups are no longer in a state to be reused, these can be given back to the start-up for recycling. Even if you throw these away, you can be guilt-free as they are biodegradable.

114. Handful, but a Cleaner Step Forward

What you see below look like common products that are easily available in the market. However, these are different. Some companies have made it their mission to reduce the waste in our oceans by creating products using waste materials like ocean plastic. Though a handful, these innovative products include.

1. Backpacks made of cyclepond fabric which is made from recycled commercial fishing net.
2. Skateboards made from recycled fishnets.
3. Bottles made with a blend of recovered ocean plastic and post-consumer recycled plastic.

115. Invasive Water Hyacinth

A very common sight on ponds and lakes are floating plants with thick, glossy leaves bearing beautiful lavender-pink flowers with six petals, the top one having a distinctive yellow-orange spot on it. The hanging fibrous roots of this plant are feathery and purplish-black. These are water hyacinth plants. They are one of the fastest-growing plants known. They reproduce very fast and their population can double in a fortnight. When not controlled, they very quickly cover the entire surface of lakes and ponds. This significantly affects marine life by blocking sunlight to submerged plants, and starving the water of oxygen, often killing wildlife such as fish and other aquatic animals.

Water hyacinth is popular for its beauty and tropical appearance but steps should be taken to control it before the plant becomes a menace and takes over entire water bodies.

116. Beat the Hyacinth

Attitude is everything! Water hyacinth is considered to be the worst aquatic weed in the world. It is quite expensive to remove this weed. Therefore, instead of removing this weed maybe we try and turn it into a fantastic bio resource.

- Hyacinth is edible. It is 17% fibre, 36% carbohydrate, 80 % protein, and it has vitamins B1 & B2.
- The pretty flowers, young glossy leaves, of water hyacinth can be eaten, boiled or fried.
- It can be fed to farm animals and they can replace their expensive protein supplements. Cows, goats, chickens, turkeys and ducks, can have this as their primary food.
- It can also be fed to biogas plants to produce methane gas, used as fuel.
- The extremely long, fibrous, feathery roots of the plant increase the surface area, hence significantly improving its absorbing capability.
- Water hyacinths are extremely tolerant of heavy metals and can absorb large amounts of them. They can also remove toxic materials such as cyanide from water. This makes the plant a possible resource for bio-cleaning industrial waste.
- Dried stalks of the water hyacinth plant are used as an excellent fibre source for making furniture, mats and artefacts.

117. Protect Peatlands

Peatlands are a type of wetland where owing to high levels of humidity and the soggy environment dead plant materials do not fully decompose. In these ecosystems, peat builds up as spongy dark soil that's sometimes referred to as sod or turf. Over thousands of years, thick layers of peat accumulate and trap huge amounts of carbons, helping to cool the climate on a global scale. It is estimated that a billion tons of carbon could be emitted from peatlands; an amount equivalent to about 10 years of emissions from all human activities, including burning fossil fuels and clearing forests. Unless steps are taken to protect peatlands, carbon loss could accelerate. The first step, however, is to raise awareness around the world of this precious natural resource and the consequences of continuing to exploit it.

118. Local Plantation

Planting trees is still one of the best ways to counter climate change. While planting new plants, it is best to take into account the natural climate and the need of the area. We should avoid planting trees that may cause damage to the local environment. For example, Eucalyptus planted in India in the arid area, led to the water table going down further! This plant is a water guzzler. Similarly, planting pine trees in the Doon valley led to ecological challenges as the native tree was Oak.

Thus, while trees are the best solution still for climate change and we should encourage local tree planting both at the organisation and individual level.

119. Ecosystem-based Adaptation

As our planet gets hotter, we need to find better ways to adapt to the extreme weather. Coastal erosion, heatwaves and droughts are just some of the climate impacts that can be tackled using nature. One such nature-based approach is called ecosystem-based adaptation (EbA) which uses ecosystems to help people adapt to climate change. The most amazing thing about this adaptation is that it protects both people and the planet. When we use nature to defend ourselves from climate change, we also create space for plants and animals to flourish.

120. Poison Cuts Poison

Anti-venom for snakebites is made from the venom itself. Nature provides solutions for most of the problems we face. It is like a huge medicine cabinet, and the medications emerge from the flora and fauna surrounding us. Some have proven to be lifesaving. It is in our interest that we preserve and safeguard nature, so that our brilliant researchers can get a chance to find solutions that will benefit our future well-being.

Flora Fauna	Poison	Potion
Puffer fish	Pufferfish produces a deadly toxin called Tetrodotoxin which suppresses the nervous system and can cause fatal muscle paralysis. About half a dozen diners die every year from the paralysing effects of eating pufferfish, so they should not be considered food.	The toxin of the spiky pufferfish may be used to treat the chronic pain of cancer patients. Researchers have found that the toxin is 3,000 times more potent than the painkiller morphine, without the crippling side-effects of addiction and nausea.
King cobra	There is no denying that one bite of a King Cobra could kill a human.	The fatal venom could also hold the key to relieving chronic pain and the pain suffered during surgery. Researchers say that it is 20 to 200 times more potent than morphine. This poison also lacks the addictive properties of that painkiller.
Tick	Ticks are attracted to people and their four-legged pets. Once a tick buries itself in flesh, it spits saliva which is an essential bio-fluid for ticks. It dampens its host's defences and facilitates the flow of blood without any obstruction.	Researchers have found this property of tick saliva to be handy for patients whose vessels are in danger of closing up from clots. Blood-thinning drugs isolated from tick saliva are ten times more potent than the natural blood-thinning agent found in a human body.

121. Conscious Choice of Colours

If you walk into a freshly painted room, after some time the strong smell may get to you, making you feel nauseous and dizzy, and giving you a headache.

Paints have a lot of heavy metals in the pigments that are used to increase durability, maintain a fresh appearance, and resist moisture that causes corrosion. These metals, along with the biocides in the paint, are one of the main health and environmental hazards. The solvents used in conventional paints escape into the air when the paint is applied. They are given out while painting, and contribute to unhealthy indoor air, and continue to release hazardous air pollutants for up to five years, even after the brushes have dried up. This leads to respiratory and metabolic illnesses, headaches and a host of other disorders.

Having these chemicals coating our walls and in the air, what we breathe in is not desirable, especially when eco-friendly paints are available to us.

122. Tips for Earth-friendly Paints

Being eco-responsible with your choices is the best service you can do for planet Earth. So, when looking for earth-friendly paints to do up your house, please do consider certain important things.

- Make sure that the colourants/pigments/dyes used contain zero/low solvents, also known as Volatile Organic Compounds (VOCs).
- Try and avoid dark colour paints which require more paint colourants, thus increasing the levels of harmful solvents in the paint.
- Oil-based paints will have a higher VOC level than water-based paints.
- Always keep your room well-ventilated, especially when painting is in progress, regardless of the type of paint being used!

Some eco-friendly paint options are:

- Milk paints are organic, biodegradable and have zero VOC. They are non-toxic water-based paints. The typical ingredients in milk paints include clay, limestone, casein (a milk-protein) and natural earth-based pigments.
- Clay paints are VOC-free and are made from plant and mineral-based ingredients, such as oils, clays and pigments. The first thing most people notice is that they have little or no smell and cover exceptionally well.
- Lime wash is an eco-friendly paint alternative, typically made by combining a calcium-based mineral (calcium oxide, slack lime or lime) with water. It has a breathable finish, making it suitable for old and damp walls.

123. Flooded with Chemical Food

These days it is hard to get vegetables and fruits in the market, devoid of harmful chemicals in the form of pesticides. The farmers use these poisonous chemicals on their crops to keep harmful pests away. No matter how crops are handled, we are likely to consume some residue of these chemicals that remains on the food, especially when vegetables or fruits are eaten raw and not washed properly. These pesticides accumulate in our body, as most of them are not biodegradable and cause serious health issues like cancer, and damage our other vital systems. Most of the time we are not even sure of where the fruits and vegetables are grown, or sourced from, or what chemicals they are infested with. Buying organic products is a better and safer alternative, but then again, at times, just the name 'organic' also does not give us a 100 % guarantee of it being safe.

124. Community Movement

Arturo D'Souza from Goa, a former English and History teacher, started a citizen movement, known as the "Save Bondvol Lake". D'Souza noticed that the Bondvol Lake had become completely dry. It was evident that it was a human intervention that led to the drying of the lake, like the construction of new buildings.

To revive fading childhood memories, he took the lead and got the construction put on hold. When he started off, D'Souza felt clueless and alone in his efforts. But he did not give up. With persistence and focus on his mission he got the community together and went to court. The community filed a public interest petition to seek protection for the lake. The citizen efforts over the years are now close to fruition as Bondvol Lake is set to get "wetland" status.

125. Homemade Edible Paint

Children are drawn to bright colours. Playing with colours is like playing with toys. It is very important to ensure that what the children are handling is safe for them and has no toxic chemicals. Edible paints are a perfect choice for children and if these can be prepared at home, then nothing can be better.

Things needed to make edible paint:

- 4 tablespoons of cornflour (corn starch)
- Tap water
- 1 cup of boiling water
- Liquid food colouring (red, blue, green, yellow)

Preparation:

1. Mix cornflour and tap water in a saucepan to make a paste that is not too thick, nor too thin.
2. Pour in 1 cup of boiling water and stir thoroughly so that there are no lumps.
3. Heat on low fire and keep stirring till the mixture starts to change, and you will notice some clear streaks forming. Turn off the heat but continue stirring. On cooling, it thickens and turns into a custard-like consistency.
4. Divide the mixture into equal portions in empty cups and to each add a few drops of different food colours according to your requirement.
5. You can experiment by mixing two colours to get the third one. For example, to make orange, add 1 drop of red and 2 drops of yellow. To make the purple color, you can add 1 drop of blue, and add 2 drops of red.
6. The colors can be stored in the refrigerator for a few days.

Make the paint fresh, and create as many colors as you need.

126. Know the Medium to Get the Right Colour

Vegetables grow in a range of colours from beautiful white to vibrant shades of green, bright orange and deep red. The presence of certain pigments in their cells give specific colours to vegetables. To maintain these vibrant colours and textures during cooking, it is important to understand that they have to be treated differently.

Most people tend to boil vegetables vigorously until they are tender! But they land up with discoloured vegetables in the bargain, while the water used for boiling gets not only the colour but the nutrients too. That's not healthy! So, is there a way to prevent this?

To retain the colours, flavours, nutrients and textures of vegetables, try out an experiment at home and find out for yourself which medium suits which vegetable. This experiment should be done only if there is an adult to help you in the kitchen. This way, you will not have to depend on the artificial food colours which are commonly used to get the visual appeal for food. Anyway, these colours are not only harmful to our health but to the environment as well.

All you need:

- You will need three boiling pots of water. The first one has baking soda added to it to give the vegetables an alkaline boiling medium. The second pot is the control one where only water represents the neutral medium. The third pot has vinegar added to make the water acidic.
- To each pot, add a celery stick or broccoli (or any green vegetable) a peeled carrot (orange colour) and an onion (white).
- Boil for some time, observe, and compare.

Check to see:

- Is there any change in the colour and texture of the vegetable?
- In which pot has the colour of the water changed.
- Which is the pot where maximum colour and nutrients were lost?

Draw, colour and tick mark the medium suitable for the three vegetables in a chart.

127. Natural Way to Remove Harmful Substances

Regardless of the type of fruits and vegetables we buy, organic or not, it is absolutely necessary to clean them in a natural and environmentally-safe way to remove traces of any harmful diseases and chemical pesticides present on them.

Here are some natural ways to easily remove harmful chemicals at home using commonly found ingredients in the kitchen.

1. Vinegar:

- Also known as acetic acid, it is acidic in nature and hence is powerful enough to kill germs and remove pesticides from fruits and vegetables. Rinse fruits and vegetables in a tub of water with one cup of vinegar in it. Rinse again in clean water before cooking.

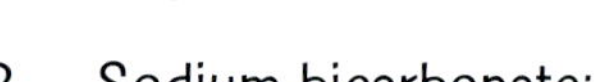

2. Sodium bicarbonate:

- Commonly known as baking soda, it is alkaline in nature and is ideal for removing harmful chemical pesticides. Soak the fruits and vegetables for 15-20 minutes in a solution made of four tablespoons of baking soda powder in five glasses of water in a large bowl. Rinse or simply wipe dry and use.

3. Turmeric:

- Turmeric is an ancient spice known for its antibacterial properties. Prepare a turmeric solution by adding five teaspoons of this yellow powder into a bowl of boiling water. Rinse the fruits and vegetables in the turmeric solution thoroughly. Rinse again in clean water and wipe dry for use.

4. Salt:

- Washing with salt water will remove most of the pesticide residues that normally appear on the surface of the vegetables and fruits.
- Solutions made of sea salts and rock salts act as natural disinfectants.
- Use one cup of salt in a bowl of water to wash the fruits and vegetables. Soak in salt water for 15 to 20 minutes. Drain, rinse and wipe for use.

The tips given above will remove most of the residue chemicals farmers use. The ideal situation is when we can all join hands and make all farmers switch to 100% organic farming and ban the use of any harmful chemicals altogether.

128. New Inventions in the Pipeline: Graphene-based Sieve

Researchers have achieved a major turning point by announcing the invention of a graphene-oxide membrane that sieves salt right out of seawater. The filter is like a mesh with holes that are so tiny that only water can pass through but not salt.

Seawater is the most abundant water resource available to us, making up 97% of Earth's water compared to only 1% of freshwater available for human drinking. The sieve can efficiently filter out salts from seawater, holding back the salts, and allowing only the water to pass through quickly and easily, thus turning seawater into clean drinking potable water.

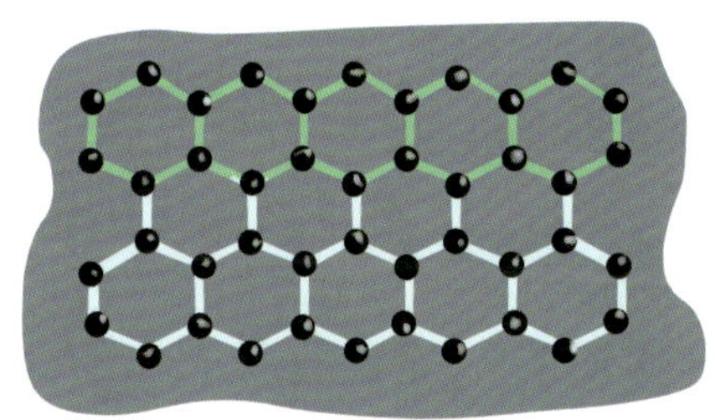

This invention is an answer to the looming water scarcity we are facing all across the globe. It can substitute the expensive energy-hogging desalination plants and quench the thirst of millions.

129. Technology: Drones Plant Trees

Trees are the longest living species on Earth. Trees are vital for storing greenhouse gas emissions, filtering air, generating water, nourishing soil, and providing food and shelter. They provide countless human services. Yet the world loses millions of trees every minute, according to the World Wide Fund for Nature (WWF).

To compensate for this, planting seeds by hand always helps, but this cannot match up to the rate at which deforestation is proceeding. So engineers and companies across the world have come up with high-tech solutions of using drones to spray tree seeds and fight deforestation. They claim that drones can plant close to a billion trees per year by spraying seeds throughout ravaged forests more quickly and efficiently than humans can do manually.

130. Technology: Satellites that Spot Methane Leaks

Methane is a powerful, greenhouse gas composed of carbon and hydrogen. While carbon dioxide is typically painted as the worst greenhouse gas, methane is roughly 30 times more potent as a heat-trapping gas.

The problem begins when unburned gas leaks and releases into the atmosphere from oil fracking and other activities giving out staggering amounts of methane for months at a time before being detected. Methane leaks and releases could undermine the greenhouse gas advantage natural gas offers and spell major trouble for the climate.

A team of scientists is trying to send a satellite into space that can pinpoint when and where methane leaks take place, so they can be plugged sooner rather than later. This will help protect the environment from methane leaks that can cause climate change.

131. Technology: Pumps to Cool Down Coral Reefs

Human activity is pouring TONS of carbon dioxide into the ocean EVERY DAY. The ocean is becoming too warm and too acidic for aquatic organisms to live. One such species we are losing at an alarming rate are our beautiful colourful flowers of the oceans, namely the coral reefs which are of enormous economic value not only to us but also the vast aquatic ecosystem. A rise in sea water temperature is enough to affect the coral reefs. They protect coastal cities from storms and support fisheries. Reefs are highly sensitive to heat increases. One-fourth of all marine species spend some part of their lifecycle in the coral reef ecosystem. If the coral reefs go extinct, so will the other species that depend on them and eventually, it will destroy the entire food chain.

132. Tropical Forest of the Ocean

Coral reefs are like underwater cities, inhabited by thousands of species, built up by the calcium carbonate skeletons of corals.

So how can we stop the destruction of coral reefs? One thing that we can do at our level is to deal with localised threats. Pollution is the main threat to corals. We need to focus on removing plastic bags and fishing gear from corals, which are choking the reefs.

Researchers and scientists have proposed several remedies such as floating shades to block the sunlight that aggravates bleaching, cooling reefs with cold water pumped up from the deep ocean, altering the chemical composition of seawater, and counteracting ocean acidification.

133. Organic Bags

The bags in the picture look like they are made of plastic, but they are not. They are organic bags. Ashwath Hegde from Bangalore has developed them, and they take less than 180 days to biodegrade. They can be burnt without releasing poisonous dioxin gases and they dissolve in water in a matter of seconds. They are made from natural starch that is freely available in plants, and also from vegetable oil and vegetable waste. These ingredients are safe, and eco-friendly. They will not harm the cows when they rummage through garbage and consume packets along with kitchen waste. After four years of extensive research, Hegde founded his company 'Envigreen' that produces special organic bags.

India faces a massive plastic problem, with tons of plastic waste generated every day. Several cities and states have tried to tackle the issue by banning single-use plastic items but people are so accustomed to plastic that they find it hard to live without. If more companies like Envigreen join hands together, then the solution might be in the organic bags.

134. Clean Environment for Healthy Cells

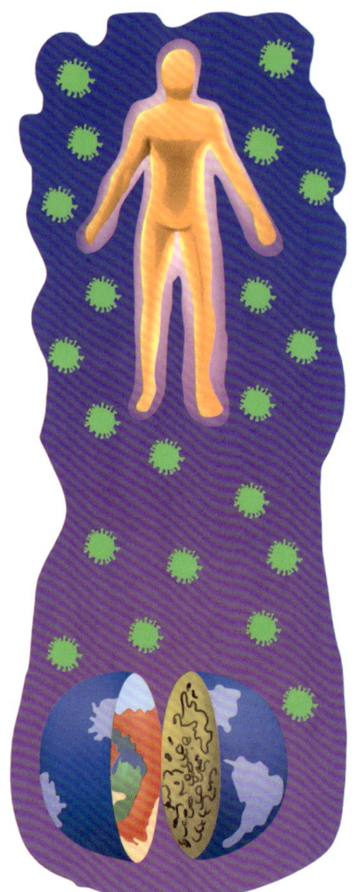

Burning plastics especially in landfills that catch fire, releases poisonous neurotoxins, and pollutes the air. This in turn affects the brain with its 100 billion neurons and 60 million sensory receptors.

On the other hand, releasing 800ml of sweat every day is one of the many ways our body throws out toxins to stay healthy. On an average, in one's lifetime, the body also produces 23,000 litres of saliva which can actually fill up a swimming pool, but a few drops of infected spit can cause havoc by spreading contagious diseases. Hence, No Spitting in public.

135. If Mosquitoes Were to Disappear...

Mosquitoes have perfectly integrated with their ecosystems by existing for the last 100 million years. There are nearly 3,500 species of mosquitoes that exist, and if they were all to disappear the consequences would be harmful. Mosquitoes are an important food source for migratory birds, other insects, reptiles, amphibians and fish everywhere. If this food chain is disrupted, it will impact the species dependent on it. If we eradicate mosquitoes, the ecosystem where they are active will die out eventually, and other insect populations would increase and replace them as pollinators or food sources.

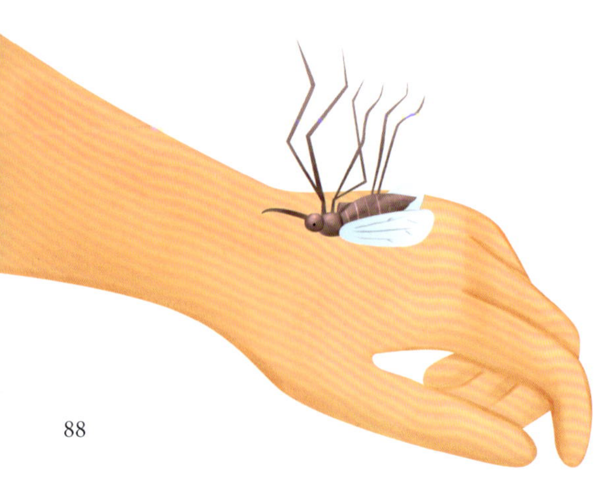

136. 'Sponge City'

In recent years, climate change has made extreme storms more common in El Salvador. They last over a few days, causing extensive damage and landslides.

But a movement is underway to create a 'natural' defence against floods, where city officials and coffee farmers, with support from UNEP, have launched project 'CityAdapt' to restore 1,150 hectares of forests and coffee plantation's ability to absorb rainfall. Trees and other vegetation can be used as sponges, drawing enormous quantities of water into the earth, preventing erosion, limiting floods and recharging groundwater supplies for times of drought.

The term 'sponge city' is used to describe urban areas around the world that are using nature-based solutions and innovative strategies to create green spaces to tackle flooding.

137. Adaptation Holds the Key

The year 2020 not only devastated the world with Covid 19, but was also the year of record temperatures. Very hot climates have become a norm and in turn lead to high temperatures, floods, droughts, storms, wildfires and even locust plagues. Even more worryingly, the Paris Agreement target to limit global warming to below 2 degrees celsius this century is slipping further away. The world is warming up and we are heading for at least a 3°C temperature rise this century.

For the sake of our planet, people must work together to plan, finance and implement change.

138. Destructive Human Behaviour

Destructive human behaviour has a severe impact on the environment. Read the following facts to know more.

- Humans use over 31% of the land area of the planet for grazing farmed animals.
- Humans use over 20% of the land area of the planet for managed forestry.
- Humans extract five times as much food from the Earth for farmed animals than for themselves.
- Humans catch and kill trillions of sea animals each year.
- Humans pour over a billion tons of toxic chemicals into the environment each year.

Look at the difference in impact on the environment if everyone ate vegan meals instead of conventional meals.

Organic Vegan Meal	Conventional Meal
1.5 million tons of organic plant foods served	9 million tons of conventional foods served.
Can restore millions of acres of forests	Destroys thousands of acres of forests
Can save gallons of fresh water	Degrades millions of acres of land

139. Majuli Island

Majuli Island on the Brahmaputra river, India was once a flourishing land for wildlife, a land of plenty. But people started to cut down trees to earn quick money, and soon the land turned barren. This transformation was witnessed by Jadav Payeng who grew up there. It pained him, and he decided to do something about it rather than be a passive spectator. He walked to a spot in the middle of the barren landscape and planted the first tree. Henceforth, he never looked back and for 37 years he planted trees daily on a routine basis without fail. The result was incredible! The forest returned, so did the wild animals. A herd of hundred elephants, along with tigers, rhinos and deer, now live in the forest that he rejuvenated with sheer determination and dedication. Thanks to Jadav, 1,359 acres of sandbanks of Majuli Island are now a true tropical paradise.

140. Cookware to Avoid: Aluminium Cookware and Aluminium Foils

Aluminium is widely used as it is very strong, versatile, lightweight and recyclable. However, as cookware, it is not without hidden dangers. High levels of aluminium in the body lead to several nervous-system related diseases including Alzheimer's. Aluminium cookware is usually coated, but the coating is prone to chipping, allowing the toxins to leach into the food.

As for aluminium foil, using it while cooking is even more dangerous especially when it is wrapped around the food and heated at a high temperature. A significant amount of aluminium leaches into the food much higher than the permissible level. The worst is if it is cooked in an acidic medium by adding lemon, it starts aggressively breaking down layers and layers of aluminium, letting it seep into the food. It is alright to wrap cold food and leftovers in it, but avoid heating food wrapped in aluminium foil.

141. Cookware Caution: Copper

Nobody can deny the richness and beauty of shining copper pots especially when pans are seen in the glossy photos of kitchens in a home decor magazine.

Many professional chefs prefer to use copper pans because of their superior heat conductivity. But copper is highly reactive, as the metal easily dissolves with some foods. Intake of large amounts of copper can cause one to suffer from extremely unpleasant symptoms of nausea, vomiting, diarrhoea and metal poisoning. According to the Food and Drug Administration, acidic foods cause copper or unprotected cookware to dissolve into foods. Tin wears out easily, and needs to be replaced every few years, which is why it is better to buy copper pots lined with stainless steel. These are more expensive than tin-lined ones but at least they last longer.

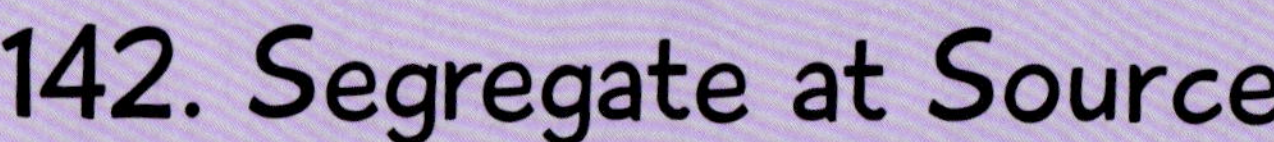

142. Segregate at Source

When you sit at the dinner table, look at all the food on it carefully. Then list out the things on the table that can be put into a compost pit to get back rich compost used as plant fertilizer. Also, list out the things that should not be put into the compost pit but instead should be sent straight to the recycler to avoid dumping and reaching the landfills. Better still, think about ways in which these can be reused before recycling.

143. Cookware with Caution: Stainless Steel

Stainless steel is a relatively safe alternative. It is a great cookware option that is long-lasting, lightweight, scratch-resistant and comes in non-stick varieties. Just make sure it is food-grade stainless steel with NO nickel or chromium.

- Nickel is a toxic element. Exposure to nickel can lead to damage to the liver and kidney, leading to high blood pressure, heart disease and an increased risk of lung cancer.
- Chromium toxicity causes severe gastrointestinal irritation or ulcers, nausea, vomiting, diarrhoea, fever and other complications.

144. More Cookware with Caution: Ceramic-coated Cookware

Ceramic-coated cookware is safe for cooking. However, ceramic-coated cookware usually hides pretty nasty stuff in it, as the soft ceramic coating is not durable enough to last and soon develops cracks and chips after a few months of use. When this happens, lead and cadmium which are found in the coating will end up in the body via the food. Lead poisoning is one of the most dangerous types of metal poisoning that can cause health complications like abdominal pain and headache, among others. As for cadmium, it is toxic even in the tiniest amounts, causing a severe deformity. Even if the ceramic-coated cookware is devoid of lead and cadmium, it can still cause danger to us when it gets chipped, because it is usually coated over neurotoxic aluminium pans. So, go for 100% ceramic cookware, which is safe as it is made of completely natural materials.

145. Old Is Gold: Cast-iron Cookware

Here are non-toxic cooking ware options that have truly withstood the test of time.

Cast-iron: Although cast-iron cookware was invented centuries ago, it is becoming popular again and is the preferred choice over modern-day cookware in restaurants and homes. The reasons are simple.

- The cast-iron poses no health risks, and can be heated to extremely high temperatures without negative effects.
- It does not leak anything toxic into the food, and is a natural way to increase the body's iron level.
- It lasts forever if handled correctly.
- It is visually appealing, giving a rustic and unique feel to the presentation.
- It is highly durable and can be restored easily, even when it's completely rusted over. If we take certain precautions, it can be easily kept clean and rust-free.

146. Old Is Gold: Glassware

The beauty, functionality, and safety of glass makes it the queen of the kitchen for baking, serving and storing. Pure glassware is tried and tested, non-toxic and non-reactive. It neither releases elements into the food nor absorbs anything from it. It is easy to clean and can offer superior baking results. Though glass takes a little longer to heat, the advantage is that it also retains heat longer. This is an advantage when using it in the oven where temperatures naturally fluctuate. When the oven temperature drops a few degrees, and the heating element needs to fire up again, the glassware can keep cooking right along at the same temperature.

Clear glassware adds another benefit when baking. One can see that the ingredients are evenly distributed and monitor the progress on all sides, not just the top!

147. Seed Banking to Tossing the Ball

Normally, a seed obtained from a fruit when in contact with soil, moisture and air, may germinate at an appropriate time to form a new plant.

Our markets are flooded with varieties of fruits of various flavours and colours, which are sold commercially to customers. After enjoying the delicacy, the seeds are mainly dumped into waste bins. But think about it, isn't this a wasteful act?

What if every person keeps the seeds aside and banks them? Yes, this will give you rich rewards. Just follow these simple steps.

1. Wash and dry the seeds whose fruits you have enjoyed.
2. Wrap them with a mixture of compost and clayey soil into pre-planted seed balls of golf ball size.
3. These seed balls can be sown by depositing, and tossing them anywhere suitable for the species, or by keeping the seeds safely until the proper germination window arises.

   It is that simple, but by doing so, you can sow the seeds of hope.

148. The Groundbreaking Mycelium

Scientists use the root structure of mushrooms: mycelium, to create wondrous, versatile, incredible products that are 100% compostable alternatives to plastics, leather, styrofoam packaging, meat, and much more.

Plant-based nutritional bacon, fish and chicken meat, are grown with mycelium. They have a specific texture and flavour. They are made using a fraction of water and land to counter and replace the slaughter houses.

149. Amazon Burning

Forest is a large area covered predominantly with trees and undergrowth. But when it catches FIRE it destroys everything that comes with it. Forest fires can start from natural causes such as lightning or due to dry grass or leaves that act as fuel getting triggered by high temperature, scanty rain and dry wind factor. On the other hand, human-caused fires can be due to any number of reasons, like sparks from cut power-lines equipment or arson. Forest fire causes too much destruction, severely reducing biodiversity and contributing hugely to air pollution—the single most important global environmental risk factor for human mortality.

Human activity, especially clearing lands for farming, is the main reason why the Amazon rainforest is burning. We can help stop the rainforest burning by supporting indigenous populations by voicing their concerns and reducing our wood and paper consumption.

150. Extreme Drought and Rain

Increasing global temperatures cause water to evaporate in large amounts, which will lead to more frequent, heavy, and intense rains in the coming years. The same extra heat that causes more evaporation of ocean water, causes bigger downpours and floods and also pulls moisture even more quickly from the soil, causing longer and deeper droughts.

To reduce such extreme weather we need to stop global warming. If we do simple things like power our homes with renewable energy, switch off from the mains, reduce water wastage, buy and eat locally produced food, give up or consume less of meat, we could help save the environment. However, and the most powerful action is to SPEAK UP!

151. Eye-opening Facts

Some eye-opening facts happening around us:

1. Carbon dioxide in the atmosphere is at a record high.
2. We dump over a million metric tons of plastic into the ocean every year.
3. The area of primary forest worldwide has decreased by over 80 million hectares since 1990.
4. Earth is facing a huge shortfall in the water supply.
5. The Arctic sea ice reaches its minimum every year in September. But the September Arctic sea ice extent is declining at a rate of 13.1% per decade.

We can help reduce the impact of the adverse events by simple, doable and economical steps like:

1. Carpool or use of public transport, and resorting to cycling as far as possible.
2. Prevent TREE CUTTING and aggressively plant more and more trees and nurture them for a minimum of one year.
3. Reduce or GO PLASTIC FREE.
4. HANDLE TREAT & SAFELY DISPOSE household DRY waste and COMPOST the COMPOSTABLES.
5. Use energy-saving lights by replacing tube lights with LED bulbs. Also, use energy efficient appliances.
6. Spread awareness about harvesting.
7. Rooftop / surface rainwater to raise the ground water table, which will require less energy to lift water, reducing carbon footprint.

152. Ecofriendly Rangoli

Rangoli is a traditional Indian art form. Patterns are created on the floor using materials such as coloured rice, dry flour, coloured sand or flower petals. It is usually made during festivals. Rangolis can be of any size, from the size of a doormat to the size of an entire room. The purpose of rangoli as decoration is that it is thought to bring good luck. The designs are made from simple geometrical patterns to elaborate intricate styles depending on the skills of the individual.

Coloured powders like indigo used for cloth staining, spices like turmeric, chilli, rice flour, flour of wheat, pulses, flowers, petals, sawdust are traditionally used in the rangoli patterns, which are better than the synthetic rangoli materials available. But nothing can beat the traditional use of dry rice powder or rice paste, which gives the frosted white colour to rangolis. These natural materials are the most eco-friendly way to decorate as they serve to feed ants, insects and small birds. This shows that one must take care of other forms of life too, to create a natural balance.

153. FabBRICK

Throwing away clothing in the garbage is like throwing away valuable resources and money that will take more than 200 years to decompose in landfills. During the decomposition process, textiles generate greenhouse methane gas and leach toxic chemicals and dyes into the groundwater and soil, thus causing environmental pollution.

Clarisse Merlet, an entrepreneur and architect, has come up with a brilliant idea to make FabBRICK, bricks made from discarded garments. She mixes the textile pieces with bio-sourced, non-polluting glue that she developed. Then, this mixture is mechanically compressed in a brick mold that takes two weeks to dry naturally, thus creating no energy use.

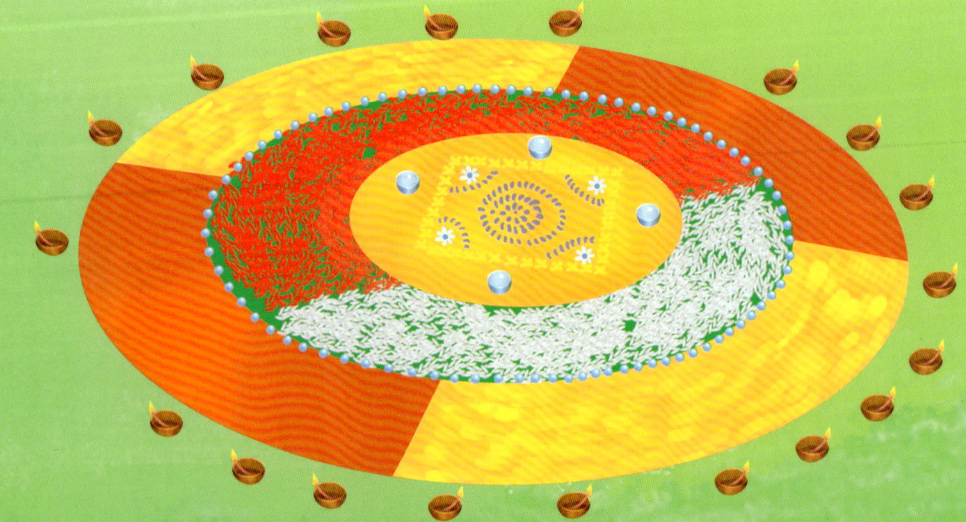

154. Rangoli Tools from Household Waste

Here are some fun ways to repurpose plastic waste for festivals.

Holes on the side of an empty plastic bottle can be made with a sharp instrument and then filled with rangoli colours to make intricate designs of multiple lines.
Old CDs can be used as stencils for round patterns.
Used cards can be used to make rangoli cones.
Used paper or plastic cups can be used by cutting out the bases and replacing them with a thin net to act as a sieve to sprinkle rangoli powder.
Old toilet cleaning bottles with a nozzle can be particularly handy to make intricate rangoli patterns.

155. Natural Cooling

It is predicted that in the years to come there will be more and more heat waves. We have a major problem at hand in the way we try to keep ourselves cool. Our air conditioning system uses tons of fossil fuels, which only makes the problem worse. It makes our houses stay cool, but the planet doesn't. But again, nature has the answer. Bringing nature into our cities can help keep temperatures down. Trees release water through their leaves, just like we cool down by sweating. Urban ponds, lakes and water bodies also help to keep the temperature lower. By using nature, we get extra benefits. Green places filter air pollution. They can be used for recreation and they are beautiful.

156. Play Games Naturally

The children wanted to play carrom, but they did not have the money to buy the expensive board that is made from wood. So, they came up with an innovative idea! They dug a shallow square trough in the soil resembling a carrom board, with all the features the game has, including pockets! They used bottle caps as strikers and carrom coins, as in the game. This brilliant idea not only saved a tree from getting chopped but also prevented waste plastic caps from polluting the environment.

Lagori, Dikori , Lagoori, Lingocha, Pithu , Palli Patti, Pitto, Pitthhu, Pittu, Satoliya, Sitolia are all different regional names for an age-old outdoor game of India. It requires a ball and a pile of seven flat stones, generally played between two teams. This no-cost, no waste, popular game is still played today in villages and towns.

157. Germany's First Hydrogen-powered Train

The world's first hydrogen-powered train was launched in Germany. The building cost of this train is more than the diesel trains, but officials say the operating costs are much lower. It runs on non-electrified train lines with low levels of noise. It emits nothing but steam and water by converting oxygen and hydrogen into electricity. If the system produces more energy than the train needs at that time, it can store the extra energy in batteries. A single tank of hydrogen can run for about 1,000 km, similar to the distance travelled by a single diesel tank. It can be refuelled in 15 minutes.

This train model is called the Coradia iLint, which was built by a French TGV maker. This move signals the beginning of efforts to move away from pollution-producing diesel trains. This is an important first step in using clean-burning technologies to reach climate protection goals. It is time other countries join them too!

158. Judicious Use of Water

Industries all over the world must resort to groundwater recharge using rooftop and surface rainwater harvesting. This will help recharge the depleting groundwater table. It will also help reduce the carbon footprint.

Reduced dependence on tanker water has other implications as well. Reduced water costs for the industry means increased profits. This can be used for improving the quality of the products and increased employment. Water that is not consumed by industrial units, can be diverted to public supply, thereby increasing water availability for citizens. Improved groundwater levels will help everyone living around the area. A reduced carbon footprint is not only helpful to the environment, but it can be used for advertising green credentials, which, in turn, can improve investments.

This can only happen if citizen groups can work together to influence government policies. Only by working together, can real change be achieved.

159. Fight the Destruction

Globally, about half a billion people rely on coral reefs for food and income from fishing and tourism. It is a well-known fact that the tsunami that hit us badly in 2004 wouldn't have caused so much destruction in the regions if the coral reefs that provide coastal defence and protection were not tampered with due to modernisation. Besides human activity, climate change is a huge risk to coral reefs. Since 2016, half of the great barrier reefs have been killed due to global warming.

The fishermen in Colombia are trying to fight the destruction of these diverse ecosystems. They are trying to repair the damaged coral reefs and grow new ones underwater. They have already transplanted the first batch of farmed corals and their hard work looks promising. The survival rate of the transplanted corals is quite high, around 85%, which gives a huge positive boost to the farmers who have taken up this noble challenge. The coral farm lies in Colombia's archipelago of San Andres and Providencia. 80% of Colombia's coral reefs are in these extensive groups of islands, which was declared a UNESCO protected marine area.

Critics say transplanting the corals alone is not enough to save the world's coral reefs. What does that mean?

160. Delicious Moringa Recipes

Moringa is put on a pedestal as a superfood. The super healthy leaves and flowers of Moringa are perfect ingredients for creating seriously yummy bites. They are great for making immune-boosting moringa smoothies, creamy moringa latte and even moringa pancakes. You can even mix delicious bites of green moringa leaves with pumpkin seed cupcakes or with ice-cream. These recipes are sure to leave you wanting a little more without feeling like you ate all your calories for the day.

161. Benefits of Sattu

Alimentary boon Superfood

Sattu is packed with insoluble fibre, which is considered to be an effective tool to keep the walls of our stomachs and intestines healthy. It also helps to remove grease from greasy food. It controls bloating, constipation and acidity.

Glowing hair

The rich insoluble fibre content in sattu absorbs and retains a lot of water. Due to this property, it helps to hydrate the body, especially during summer. As a result of this, the moisture content of the skin improves, giving it a glow. Traditionally, sattu has also been used to treat hair problems. Rich in iron, it helps to reduce hair fall and improves the quality of hair by increasing the oxygen flow to the hair roots.

Superfood Coolers

Sattu can be used to make the perfect summer cooler drink which not just provides calmness to the body during the heat, but also protects against sunstrokc.

This cooler can be sweet or salty depending on your preference. The salty drink is made with sattu, onion, lemon juice, black salt, cumin powder, and water. This drink has a tangy and spicy taste. For making the sweet version, take a glass of milk, add two tablespoons of sattu powder, one teaspoon sugar and mix well. It's cheap and easy to prepare but is getting recognised as a rich health drink. Better late than never!

Slow absorbing carbohydrates

Carbohydrates are essential for our body, but not all carbohydrates have equal effects. Some carbohydrates are more slowly digested, absorbed and metabolised and cause a lower and slower rise in blood sugar levels.

Sattu is one of these slow absorbing carbohydrates and hence it is good for diabetic people. Health experts recommend consuming sattu daily to keep the blood sugar levels under control, regulate blood pressure, while the high fibre content controls high cholesterol issues too.

162. Help Trees to Help Us

Trees matter, and we should be looking after them. To fully use their powers, trees need our help. Here are five reasons that explain why:

1. Trees regulate the water cycle.
2. Trees are a vital habitat for wildlife.
3. Trees improve the soil quality and filter our water, making the drinking supply cleaner and more reliable.
4. Trees prevent soil erosion.
5. Trees fight climate change by absorbing greenhouse gases.

163. Controlling Sewage

Putting a simple net at the mouth of the outlet drain to filter out the plastics and other solid pollutants is just a primary treatment. But think about it as a simple, yet brilliant way to prevent waste from flowing out into water bodies and then trying to clean the mess from the vast rivers, seas and oceans. What do you think?

164. What If?

Forests are the lungs of the world. They give oxygen to us and act as a giant sponge, sucking up tons of the planet's carbon dioxide emissions every year and also work as a huge air conditioner for a warming world. But what would happen if they were replaced?

That's right! Cutting down large swathes of dense forests to allow more room for cattle pastures, hand over to the soy producers and even open up the magnificent forests to mining spells disaster for our environment.

At the end, who will really suffocate? Environmentalists fear that the lungs of the planet will be sacrificed for the interests of agribusiness.

165. Natural Defence from Drought

Drought is a major impact of climate change, and scientists predict it will become more common over the coming years. Especially in poor parts of the world where many people still rely on rains for farming, food security gets threatened. The trees and wetlands act as sponges, absorbing water and recharging ground water supplies. So, when we cut down trees, droughts get worse because rain flushes straight through the soil instead of being stored for times of need. But when we keep our forests and rivers healthy, we are also protecting our water supplies.

There is no need to choose between nature or people, now, it is nature for people.

166. Effects of Global Warming

The effects of global warming are obvious around us. Be it the rising sea levels, melting of glaciers and ice sheets, or warming of the ocean surface, all these factors lead to an increase in temperature. Surprisingly, it is only a handful of people who are concerned and talking about it while most have an indifferent attitude, thinking it is a phase that will pass. Will it?

Here are some of the most unexpected ways climate change impacts the smallest to the largest components of the Earth.

- Bacteria are found everywhere, especially in soil. The colonies of bacteria can grow so thick that they form layers of crust that protect the soil against erosion. This is seen in desert soil too. Though they may appear bare and devoid of life, different types of desert bacteria thrive in different temperatures and help to protect the soil. But temperatures have become erratic and with climate change it is a struggle for the desert bacteria to keep up with the change and adapt, leaving desert soil more prone to erosion.

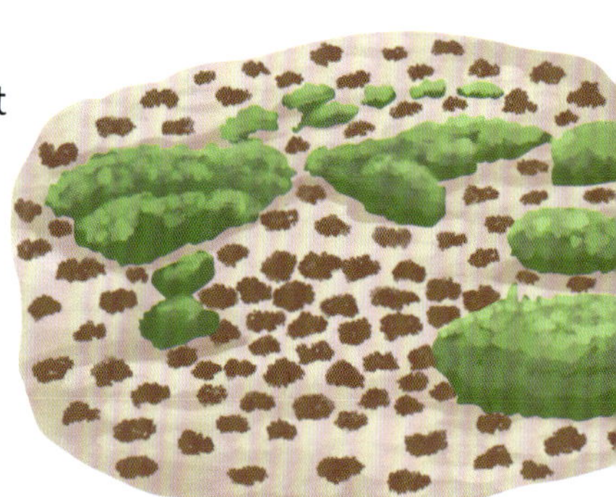

- Volcanic eruptions

Presently, 10 per cent of the land area on Earth is covered with glacial ice, including glaciers, ice caps, and the ice sheets of Greenland and Antarctica.

As glaciers melt and flood into oceans, and the global sea-level rises with climate change, the distribution of weight on the Earth's crust will shift from land to sea. Studies suggest that this shift in weight distribution could eventually over a while cause volcanoes to erupt more often.

- Oceans darken

Cloudbursts and downpours have become more common in certain parts as a result of climate change. Increased precipitation results in stronger currents, stirring up more silt and debris, which eventually flows into the oceans, making them murkier and darker. Coastal regions of Norway have already experienced this in recent decades. Some researchers have speculated that the murkiness is responsible for changes in regional ecosystems, including a boom in jellyfish populations since they have a unique lifecycle where they can tolerate harsh conditions and then rapidly thrive when conditions are favourable.

- Allergies worsen

The incidents of allergies in the world are increasing. One of the main factors for this is climate change. As global temperature and carbon dioxide levels rise, plant pollination cycles have become longer and more intense. This increases the overall pollen load each year, making people's allergies worse with passing time.

- A slowdown in ant invasions

Researchers have estimated that 18.5 per cent of the land on Earth currently supports the big-headed ant (BHA). But as temperatures shift in the coming decades, the habitat range of these cold-blooded animals will likely shrink substantially. Some climate models suggest that the ant's range will decrease by one-fifth by the year 2080. How native insects will respond to these changes, however, remains unclear.

- Sunlight floods polar seafloor

As sea ice melts, more sunlight will penetrate the shallow coastal regions around the poles. Sea organisms such as worms, sponges, and others accustomed to existing in darkness will begin to experience longer periods of sunlight with each successive summer. This alteration will significantly affect them as excess sunlight will allow the marine plants to grow rapidly and take over the habitat from them. This transition has already been observed in pockets of both the Arctic and Antarctic coastlines, and could significantly decrease biodiversity in these regions.

167. Grow Your Fresh Air

Green plants are the lungs of the Earth: they produce the oxygen that makes life possible, add precious moisture, and filter all the toxins that human activity generates. We do not have to buy those fancy expensive gadgets that run on electricity claiming to purify toxic air. We can create an impactful, low-cost, breathable environment by just growing simple houseplants in one's home or office with the same efficiency as the rainforest does. These houseplants are the best filters of the common poisonous chemical pollutants, such as ammonia, formaldehyde and benzene, trapped in unventilated rooms where we spend most of our time in.

For really efficient results, don't forget to declutter your rooms, and as far as possible remove artificial artefacts. Go for natural ones and select the right plants for your rooms, and let them do what machines cannot. If you are surrounded by plants, you will notice incidents of headache, asthma, eye irritation and breathing problems will reduce drastically and you will always feel energised. So try purifying the air in your home with these plants:

Areca palm	These trees are good for the living room corners.	Areca palm also emits large amounts of water vapour. The plant is tolerant of most indoor environments.
Mother-in-law's tongue plant or Sansevieria plant	A must for the bedroom at night, this plant absorbs carbon dioxide and releases oxygen, keeping the air fresh all through. They need to be wiped clean regularly to keep their stomata free from dust.	This plant is very hardy, being able to tolerate almost any condition and still grow. It excels at removing formaldehyde, benzene, and trichloroethylene from the home or office.
Money plant	This is one of the best plants to grow in shade.	Keep as many as you want as this plant can grow easily in water by simply placing a cutting. It is also a great way to get rid of benzene and formaldehyde in your home.
Rubber plant	This evergreen tree is an excellent indoor plant.	The rubber plant is especially effective at removing carbon monoxide and formaldehyde from indoor air.

168. Whose Responsibility?

Cities all over the world create huge urban garbage. While cities do have sewage systems to deal with this garbage, in reality, more than this amount goes untreated into the rivers or water bodies. But there has been massive pollution of rivers on a global level which has a strong impact on our ecosystem. This has been caused by the increasing demand for water bodies and population explosion.

So, what do you think? Does the onus to keep rivers clean lie only with the government, and can we really carry on the way we have been doing for years?

169. Converted Conditioner

In the hot and sticky summer, air conditioners are a breezy saviour. The dependence on these energy guzzlers is increasing as the mercury keeps rising due to climate change. But now researchers say they have a solution for these energy hogs that actually helps the climate. They are working on a way to use air conditioning units to capture carbon dioxide straight from the atmosphere and transform it into fuel. The idea is that these renewable-energy powered devices would lower atmospheric CO2 and provide a scalable alternative to oil, natural gas and other fossil fuels.

It's all theoretical for now, but the conversion technology for each step of the process already exists, where CO2 and water from the air are first taken up. Then, it is passed through an electric current that splits the water into hydrogen and oxygen. Finally, combining the hydrogen with the captured CO2 produces hydrocarbon fuel.

Researchers are working on a complete system that will put all of the pieces together to make it a functional unit to capture CO2 from the air and make substantial and relevant amounts of hydrocarbon fuels.

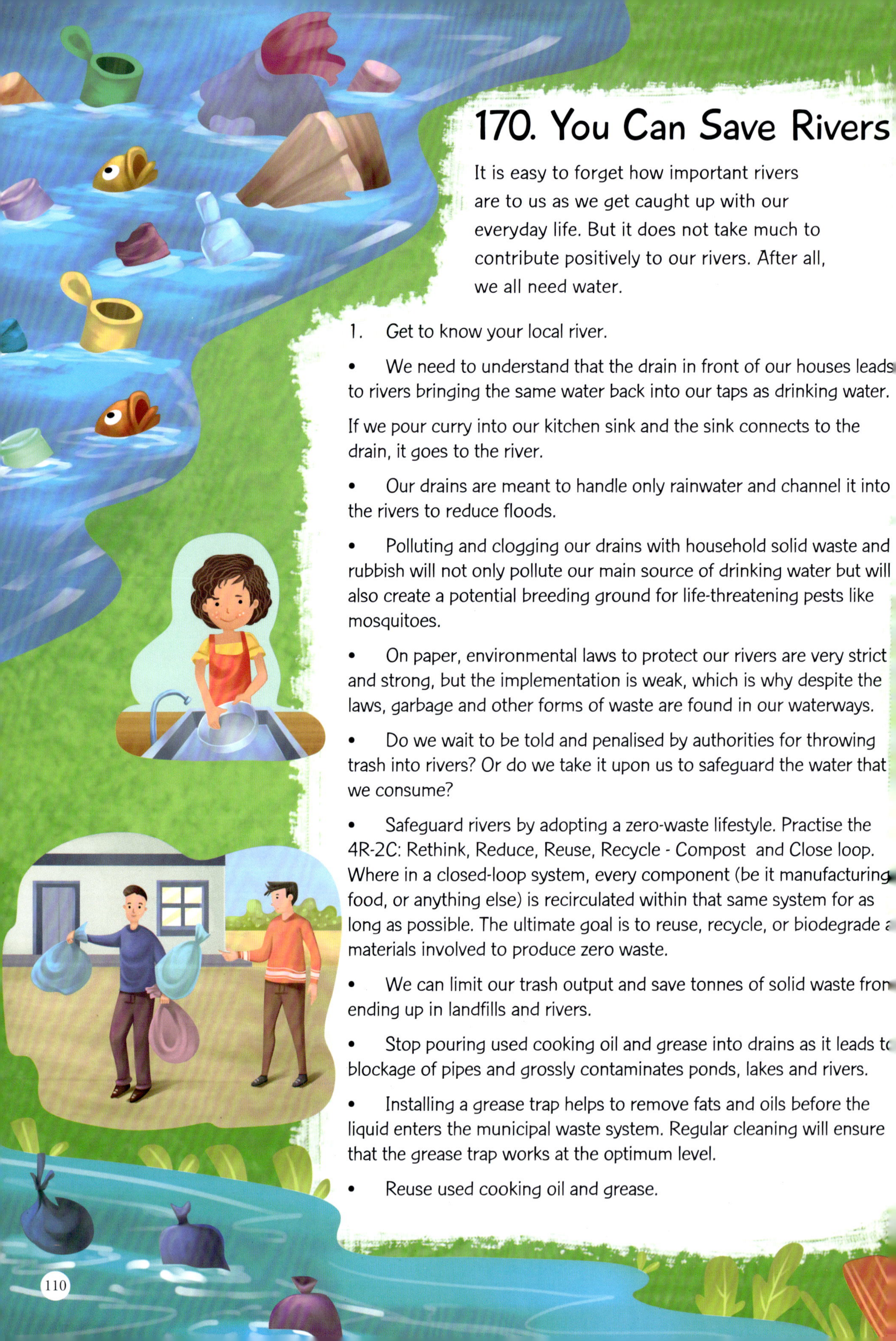

170. You Can Save Rivers

It is easy to forget how important rivers are to us as we get caught up with our everyday life. But it does not take much to contribute positively to our rivers. After all, we all need water.

1. Get to know your local river.

- We need to understand that the drain in front of our houses leads to rivers bringing the same water back into our taps as drinking water.

If we pour curry into our kitchen sink and the sink connects to the drain, it goes to the river.

- Our drains are meant to handle only rainwater and channel it into the rivers to reduce floods.
- Polluting and clogging our drains with household solid waste and rubbish will not only pollute our main source of drinking water but will also create a potential breeding ground for life-threatening pests like mosquitoes.
- On paper, environmental laws to protect our rivers are very strict and strong, but the implementation is weak, which is why despite the laws, garbage and other forms of waste are found in our waterways.
- Do we wait to be told and penalised by authorities for throwing trash into rivers? Or do we take it upon us to safeguard the water that we consume?
- Safeguard rivers by adopting a zero-waste lifestyle. Practise the 4R-2C: Rethink, Reduce, Reuse, Recycle - Compost and Close loop. Where in a closed-loop system, every component (be it manufacturing food, or anything else) is recirculated within that same system for as long as possible. The ultimate goal is to reuse, recycle, or biodegrade a materials involved to produce zero waste.
- We can limit our trash output and save tonnes of solid waste from ending up in landfills and rivers.
- Stop pouring used cooking oil and grease into drains as it leads to blockage of pipes and grossly contaminates ponds, lakes and rivers.
- Installing a grease trap helps to remove fats and oils before the liquid enters the municipal waste system. Regular cleaning will ensure that the grease trap works at the optimum level.
- Reuse used cooking oil and grease.

171. Creative Uses of Used Cooking Oil

Using the same cooking oil for repeated frying has adverse health effects. In homes, simply disposing of cooking oils down the drain is a bad idea. The oil will harden in the drain and cause a clog. If allowed to enter the natural environment, it pollutes the water bodies.

We can use simple household reused cooking oil as:

1. Household lubricant for squeaking hinges to troublesome locks.
2. Fuel for oil lamps.
3. Helping to remove paint from our hands. Rub the used oil on your hands and let it sit for five minutes. Then wash your hands and the paint will come off.

172. All We Need Is...'Magical Peel'!

Citrus, Mango, Banana, Melon,
These fruity delights, are simply heaven.
Hope you don't chuck the inedible peels.
Do you know they have magical powers to heal?
Just like the way you prepare any meal,
You can do the same with any kind of peel.
Recycling the garbage peels at home, is the need of the hour.
For those in a rush, sprinkle a few granules of dry yeast.
Changes the ninety-day process to thirty days at least.
An organic cleanser, multi-use for growth and care.
An ideal choice to replace all home toxic chemicals in compare.
It not only removes dirt, stains, odour and the pest,
Also, magically decontaminates the environment, they are the best!
Switching to Bio-Enzyme, is very sensible, I feel;
All We Need Is..... brew your own "Magical Peel".

"Water and air, the two essential fluids on which all life depends, have become global garbage cans."

- Jacques Yves Cousteau

"Even among the trash, the seeds chose **LIFE!!!!** Never underestimate the power of **CHOICE**."

"Enjoy the fruits, sow its seeds and hope for the Best!"

"Devote 100 hours every year towards the cause of cleanliness".

- Swachh Bharat Abhiyan Slogan

173. Vulnerable Small Islands

Small islands are particularly vulnerable to the effects of climate change because of their low lying, ocean-fronted borders, relatively small land masses, and exposure to extreme weather and climate variability. To put it simply, small islands are more vulnerable to climate change because there is nowhere to go as the sea rises, nowhere to hide when extreme weather events such as hurricanes arrive. Most small islands cannot afford to do much about climate change so we should all join with them and be particularly vocal in international forums about the need to take action to reduce greenhouse-gas emissions.

174. Swallowed by Sea

Once proud of a coastline of 480 kms, the people of the state of Odisha in India are now wary of the disaster it awaits. Over 100 kilometres(km) out of the state's 480km long coastline are facing erosion. Many villages have been the victims of the wrath of the ocean, almost at regular intervals and continuously.

Once, proud owners of rich, sprawling paddy fields ,these residents have either migrated or have been forced to change their livelihood from farming to fishing.

175. Pull Carbon Out of the Sky

Today, airplanes pump a lot of climate-warming carbon dioxide into the atmosphere. But someday, carbon dioxide sucked from the atmosphere could be used to power airplanes. Researchers are working on a simple, yet world-altering method by using a new iron-based catalyst to suck CO2 from the air into airplanes where it is converted directly to jet fuel. Unlike cars, planes can't carry batteries big enough to run on electricity from wind or solar power. But if CO2, rather than oil, were used to make jet fuel, that could reduce the air travel industry's carbon footprint — which currently makes up 12 percent of all transportation-related CO2 emissions. This carbon-neutral flight would represent a massive step towards addressing the climate crisis by not only removing greenhouse gases from the atmosphere but also our sole dependence on fossil fuel.

176. Earthy Red Clay

Today people take pride to set up solar panels and rainwater harvesting structures at their home and office buildings, but when it comes to modern construction we continue to use materials like cement, glass and marble elsewhere. Why couldn't people associate sustainable materials like mud and timber with modern apartments? Take the refurbished earthy red clay tiles, for instance, which are far superior as they are designed to withstand extreme weather conditions like heat and rain. They are insect-resistant, fireproof, and have a longer lifespan than conventional plastic ones. This will encourage and give revenue to local artisans and potters to keep their traditional practices alive and continue using local construction materials to produce aesthetics with modern designs. Take the first step by replacing plastic plant pots with earthen pots as they retain water for a longer period and even make the air cooler for plants to thrive in them.

177. Organic Photovoltaics

Sunlight offers a potential solution in the search for an energy source that does not harm the planet, to efficiently turn electromagnetic energy into electricity. Researchers from the Saudi Arabian research university KAUST have shown how a known herbicide can improve this conversion in organic devices. Organic materials are starting to break through as an alternative to the traditionally used silicon solar cells because they are light, flexible and relatively inexpensive to make, even offering the possibility for printable manufacture. For organic photovoltaics to become a realistic replacement for fossil fuels, they must improve their efficiency when converting the fraction of solar energy to electrical energy. The key to achieving this is choosing the right combination of materials which the scientists are working on.

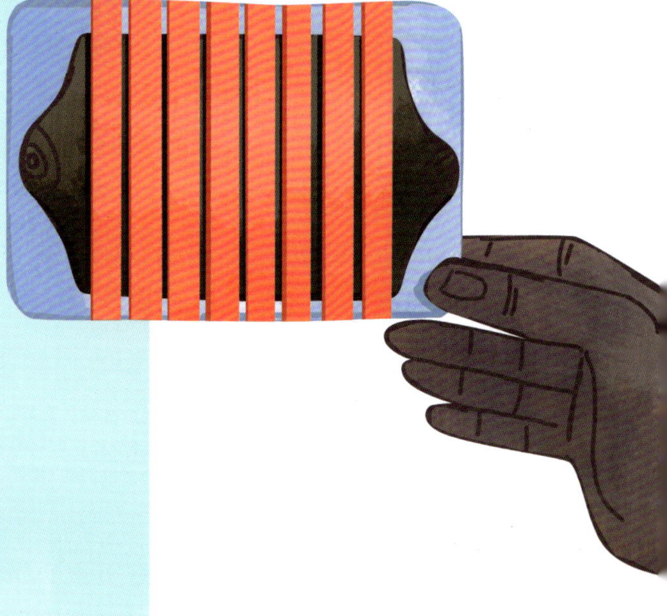

178. Invisible Energy

Years after the COP 21 Paris Climate Agreement, all eyes are on the world's progress on the road to a carbon-free future. Solar energy has always held the highest hope in the scientific community, as the most reliable and abundant energy source on Earth. In recent decades, solar cells have become cheaper, more efficient, and environmentally friendly. However, current solar cells tend to be opaque, which prevents their wider use and integration into everyday materials, constrained to being lined up on roofs and in remote solar farms. A new study led by scientists from Incheon National University in Korea shows how to make a fully transparent solar cell by combining the unique properties of titanium dioxide and nickel oxide semiconductors. Thus, the next-generation solar panels could be integrated into windows, buildings, or even mobile phone screens.

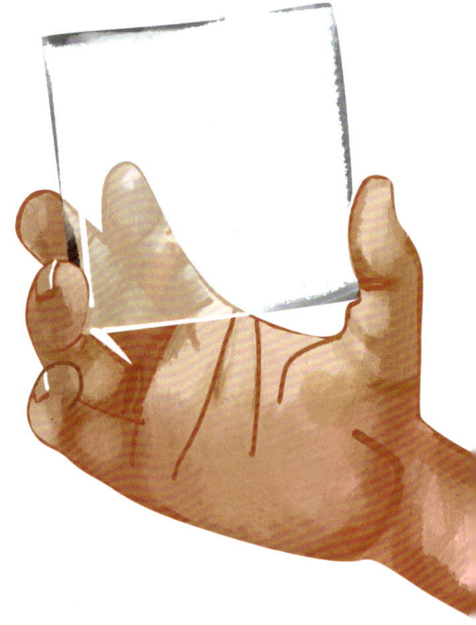

179. Biomedical Waste Disposal Guidance

Responsible HANDLING, TREATING and SAFE DISPOSAL of biomedical waste generated at home is extremely important for everyone. It can be a potential source of infection of COVID to municipal workers and other informal waste collectors, who are the second most important human shield against COVID after health workers.

BIOMEDICAL WASTE like tissues, masks, gloves, cotton swabs, bandages, gauze, sanitiser bottles, sanitary napkins, diapers, syringes, vials, etc., can be safely disposed of by following these simple steps:

- Bagged in DOUBLE layered plastic bags to avoid tearing. (Optional but preferred: YELLOW BAG / non-chlorinated plastic bags)
- Seal the mouth of the bags to avoid spilling.
- Label the bag: write/ draw/ use stickers - 'BIOMEDICAL WASTE' or use the LOGO.
- Bags to be sanitised before handing them over to the waste collector.
- Avoid throwing sharp needles directly into the bag. They should be placed in plastic or cardboard containers and marked as 'SHARPS', to avoid injuries.
- Contact nearest hospital for disposal guidance.

180. Home Quarantine Dry Waste

Every day, dry waste such as product packages, bottles, newspapers, appliances, batteries, etc., that are recyclable are thrown away from homes. These not only cause an environmental hazard when they reach the landfills but can also lead to serious health issues. If there is a suspected COVID infection in the house from which the waste is disposed of, there is a high possibility of the infection spreading.

These dry wastes can be easily kept in one corner of the house and will not cause any foul smell or disturbance. Even soiled tetra pack cartons and plastic milk packets can be washed, dried and stored away for days. Especially during a pandemic they should be HOME QUARANTINED within the home premises for an appropriate period before they are handed over responsibly to waste pickers and sent away for recycling or safe disposal.

Surfaces	Examples	Virus lives for
Metal	doorknobs, jewellery, silverware	5 days
Wood	furniture	4 days
Plastics	milk packets, plastic bottles, plastic seats, backpacks, elevator buttons	2 to 3 days
Stainless steel	refrigerators, pots and pans, kitchen sinks	2 to 3 days
Cardboard	cartons, boxes	24 hours
Copper	cookware	4 hours
Aluminium	soda cans, tin foil	2 to 8 hours
Glass	drinking glasses, measuring cups, mirrors, windows	Up to 5 days
Ceramics	dishes, pottery, mugs	5 days
Paper	mail, newspaper	varies from a few minutes to 5 days

181. Immune BOOSTER on Your plate

Food rich in core minerals and vitamins should be on our plate to boost our health and make us strong enough to fight infections such as COVID.

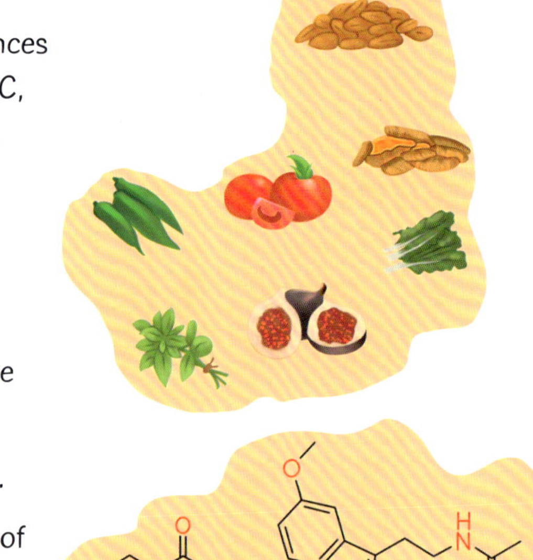

Though numerous vitamins, minerals and compounds are essential to building our immune system, the core substances that play a vital role in tackling this virus are vitamins like C, D & K along with minerals like Zinc, Magnesium, Calcium, Selenium, Quercetin.

Eggs, dairy, legumes, seeds, nuts, whole grains, shellfish, meat, fruits and vegetables are rich in different types of vitamins and minerals like Zinc, Magnesium, Calcium. Proper intake of food can provide and supplement the core substances to boost our immune system.

Selenium is present in seafood, lean meat, seeds and nuts.

Quercetin is present in red plant pigment present in skins of fruits, vegetables and grains like apples, red grapes, onions, red leaves, etc., and has potent antioxidant properties.

182. Treadle Pump

Treadle pumps work on simple stepping motion. These are very simple and inexpensive foot-operated hydraulic pumps used at shallow depths. Hence, they run without electricity and with zero operational cost. They are easy to maintain and have the advantage of being manufactured locally.

They are powered by human effort, with the upper body being stationary and the legs and feet stepping up and down on treadles that are connected to two small piston pumps.

These pumps are used extensively in rural areas for irrigation, but a few have also installed them in their homes as a means to exercise wherein the energy of mechanical effort is used to draw water and fill up the overhead tank. Besides, the water tank collects waste water from the kitchen.

183. UVC Germicidal Light

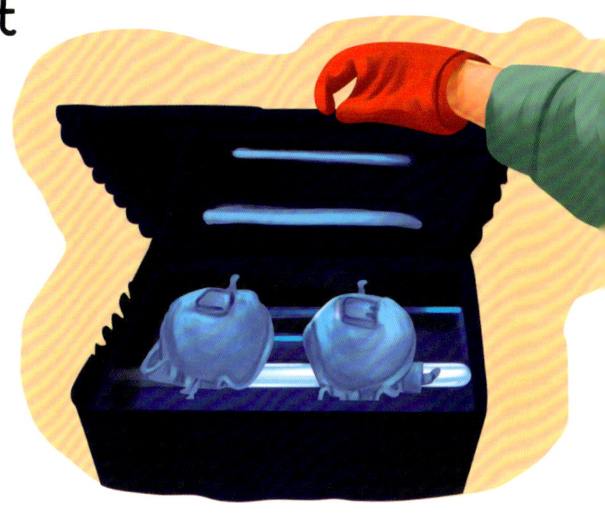

The narrow spectrum of ultraviolet light called far-UVC has a very limited range so it cannot penetrate through human skin and is not harmful to us. But in contrast, the cells of viruses and bacteria are much smaller than human cells, therefore, continuous low doses of UV-C light can reach their DNA and kill them. Thus, they are now proving to be a safer, inexpensive tool to disinfect not only hospital equipment but also public indoor areas to reduce the spread of airborne diseases.

Compared to the chemical disinfectant it has an overall advantage as it leaves no residues nor any disinfection by-products. It leaves no effects on colour, taste and odour. One does not need to store any chemicals either. It is effective against all microorganisms. The environmental impact and footprint are much smaller compared to chemical disinfectants.

184. Jal Neti (nasal cleanser)

Like brushing teeth daily cleans your teeth, using Jal Neti (nasal cleanser) daily will clean the nasal path, from the nostrils to the throat. This is a technique Yogis use to stay disease-free. With adult guidance and practice, one can use this technique to remove the dirt and bacteria trapped along with the mucus in the nostrils. A pinch of salt in lukewarm water in a Jal Neti pot is all that is required. A Neti pot is usually small and has a long spout on one side, which is small enough to be inserted gently into one of the nostrils during the process.

Now that we live in a world where information is available at the click of a button, do check out Jal Neti videos under adult supervision and note the dos and don'ts!

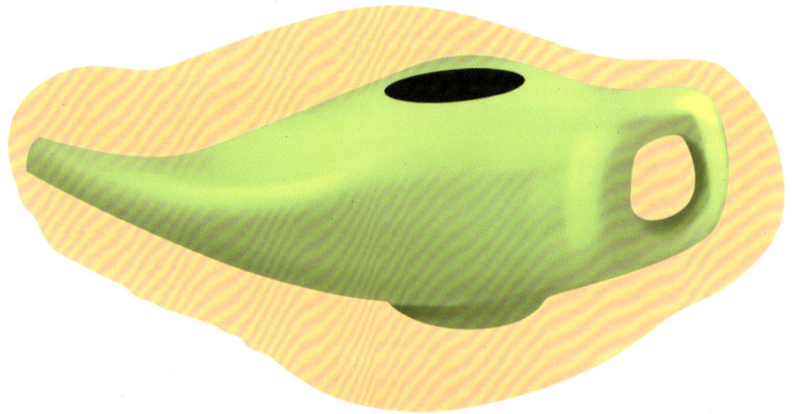

185. Food Fraud

People across the world are becoming more and more obese and sick. That is because of unhealthy choices that lurk among seemingly healthy food. Nutritional labels say things such as 'multigrain', 'no added sugar', and 'low fat'. But how do we know if these facts are correct, or we are being taken for a ride?

So, don't forget to read the nutritional label before you give a place to these foods in your kitchen cabinet. Choose wisely and fight food frauds!

186. Fruit Juice

When an option is given between an aerated drink and a fruit juice from a packet, we normally opt for fruit juice thinking it is the juice extracted from real fruits with all its nutrition intact. But that is not true. It is nothing but sugar water with added artificial colour and chemically made flavour of the fruit whose picture misleads you.

You should instead opt for fresh, cold-pressed fruit or vegetable juice, which is enriched with loads of vitamins, minerals and fibre. Fresh juice does not add non-biodegradable trash to our landfills. What is not consumed becomes compostable.

187. Health Drinks

The most common ingredients found in these drinks are corn syrup, wheat flour, salt, artificial colours, fat-reduced cocoa powder and sugar. Is that healthy?

188. Fat-free Frozen Yoghurt

A systematic comparison has shown that low-fat products contain more sugar than regular products. When manufacturers take away the fat, the flavour disappears too and so they use more sugar to make it tasty. Even if they come as low fat, they are pro fat, as they come loaded with artificial tastes, flavours, preservatives and fat-loaded toppings.

Bottom line? Don't buy low-fat products. Eat real food. The best choice is homemade yoghurt topped with fresh fruits and honey.

189. Sugar-free Food

Sugar-free does not equal healthy. When packaged food is touted as sugar-free, that often means the real sugar has been taken out and replaced with an artificial sweetener. This is a serious concern as studies have shown that these sweeteners contain dangerous hidden ingredients that are 200 times sweeter than natural sugar. This can increase your appetite, prevent weight loss and cause cancer. It is best to stick to natural sugar, but in moderation.

190. Granola Bars

Granola is a snack consisting of rolled oats, nuts, honey and other sweeteners, such as brown sugar, and sometimes puffed rice, that is usually baked until it is crisp, toasted and golden brown. Sounds good, right? But beware! What lies behind these healthy bars is nothing less than an over-processed nutritional mess. They have hidden sugar, processed ingredients like chocolate sheaths. These can be as bad as eating a candy bar or cookies containing high fructose corn syrup that can lead to increased cholesterol and diabetes.

191. Vanishing Whales

Whale hunting has increased the carbon in the atmosphere, thus accelerating climate change in the process. You must be wondering how one species has so much impact on the planet. Human beings have always worked for selfish economic gains. Whaling was one of the booming industries in the world. We had hunted them for decades for meat, extracted the oil, made perfumes from their intestines and further used their cartilage as holding threads. Somewhere along the way, the whale supply started running low and some people realised that it is not a good idea to hunt them. Whale hunting was banned in 1986, which led to a backlash. A few groups tried to oppose the move by arguing that whale hunting is good for humans, as it will leave more fish and krill for human consumption if the whales are out of the way. But on the contrary, the reverse was observed. With the vanishing of whales, the population of fish and krill also reduced significantly.

You can now imagine how vital these elegant creatures are to the planet, and how much good they might have continued to do if we had not slashed their population for decades just for lubricating machines, burning oil lamps, making perfumes and holding corsets together. It is not worth it at all!

192. Eco Wave Power

Eco Wave power is cost-effective, low maintenance, state of the art floater technology that produces clean renewable energy from ocean waves. This is delivered through cleverly designed Eco Wave floaters that can be attached to the existing man-made structures such as docks, hence making them simple and accessible for installing and maintenance. The Eco Wave floaters draw energy from incoming waves by converting the rising and falling motions of the waves into clean energy generation processes.

With one billion people reportedly lacking access to electricity and almost half the world's population living near the coastline, Eco Wave power can fill the void. A different approach from the solar, wind and other renewable energy sources – there won't be just one power source like carbon-emitting fossil fuels.

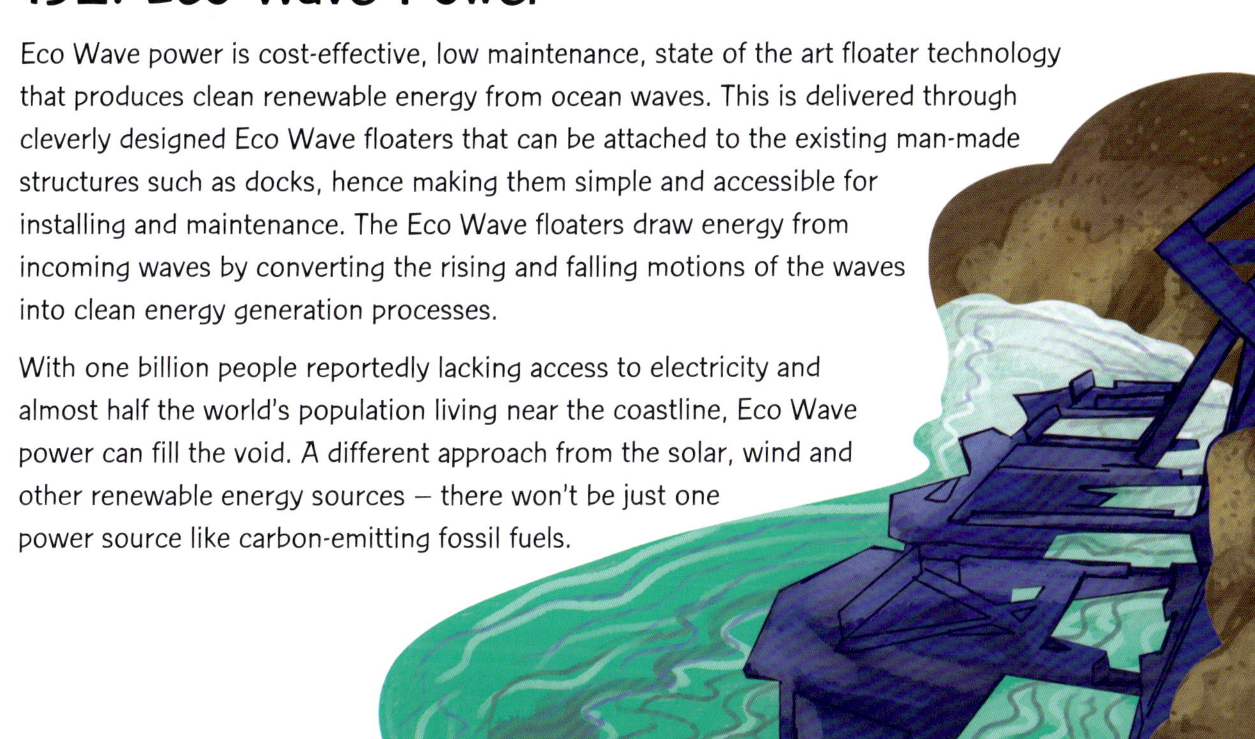

193. Whale Poop Shortages!

This is a typical case of what happens when human beings interfere with nature by removing the main predator of a food chain, leading to a trickle-down effect that can disrupt an entire ecosystem. Whales don't just eat fish and krill, they play a vital role in allowing these populations to thrive too. The whale poop released in the surface water is rich in essential nutrients like iron and nitrogen that fertilises plant plankton, which in turn is food for the krill and fish. When a whale swims up to the surface to gulp in the air for its lungs, it churns up the planktons exposing them further to the sunny surface, thus enhancing their time to reproduce. The more planktons there are in the water, the better for everyone around, not only as a source of food but also as an efficient carbon sponge, absorbing it from the atmosphere, and taking it way down to the bottom of the oceans for safe storage.

Whales directly contribute to the cause of cleaning up the atmosphere by storing a large amount of carbon in their dead bones lying on the seafloor for years, trapping and preventing the carbon to be released into the environment, preventing global warming.

Reports have shown that if the whale population would be restored to its pre-hunt levels, then huge tons of carbon can be removed from the atmosphere every year. Experts say that even after the ban of whale hunting in most countries now, we will not even reach half the level of the population that it used to be, anytime soon.

194. Khadi Prakritik Paint

India now has its own cow dung paint. Among the country's several innovative inventions, this unique paint certainly takes the cake. The 'Khadi Prakritik Paint' is a first-of-its-kind product that is being touted as eco-friendly and non-toxic, with anti-fungal and anti-bacterial properties. With actual cow dung as its main ingredient, the paint is said to be cost-effective and also odourless and has been certified by the Bureau of Indian Standards.

The paint is free from heavy metals like lead, mercury, chromium, arsenic, cadmium and others. It will be a boost to local manufacturing and will create sustainable local employment through technology transfer. This technology will increase the consumption of cow dung as a raw material for eco-friendly products and will generate additional revenue for farmers and gaushalas. The utilisation of cow dung will also clean the environment and prevent the clogging of drains.

195. Biomass to Renewable Charcoal

When wood burns incompletely, a black residue is left behind. This is charcoal.

Technically, charcoal is made from biomass through a process called pyrolysis.

The pyrolysis process involves heating biomass collected from garden waste to about 300-400 C in an environment without an oxygen supply.

The dry garden waste biomass like twigs and leaves that needs to be turned into charcoal is stacked into a pile, and completely covered – sometimes with other leafy biomass, and finally by mud. A fire is lit through a small opening, which also subsequently gets covered. These covered piles are allowed to burn for 3-7 days, after which the charcoal is taken out from the inside, in addition to some organic gases and a bio-oil, both also usable as fuels!

196. Turn Salt Water into Fresh Drinking Water

People have been trying to turn seawater into drinking water for thousands of years, but the process uses high-power pumps and is not usually energy-efficient nor affordable. At a newly constructed facility in the coastal area of Kiunga, Kenya, a nonprofit called GivePower is tackling that challenge using a solar micro-grid system, generating 75,000 liters of fresh drinking water each which is enough for 25,000 people. It relies on Tesla batteries for energy storage, and it uses two parallel pumps so that the system can run at all times, even if one pump requires maintenance. The desalination plant has already spurred new economic activity in Kiunga. A group of women there started a freshwater clothes-washing business, and others fill a tank with the water and drive it to nearby communities to sell.

197. Climate Change Report Card

Under the Paris Agreement, 196 signatory countries submitted their national plan, setting targets for emissions reductions and specifying pathways by which they aim to meet those targets.

Here are some of the leaders who have kept their promise and are working towards mitigating climate change:

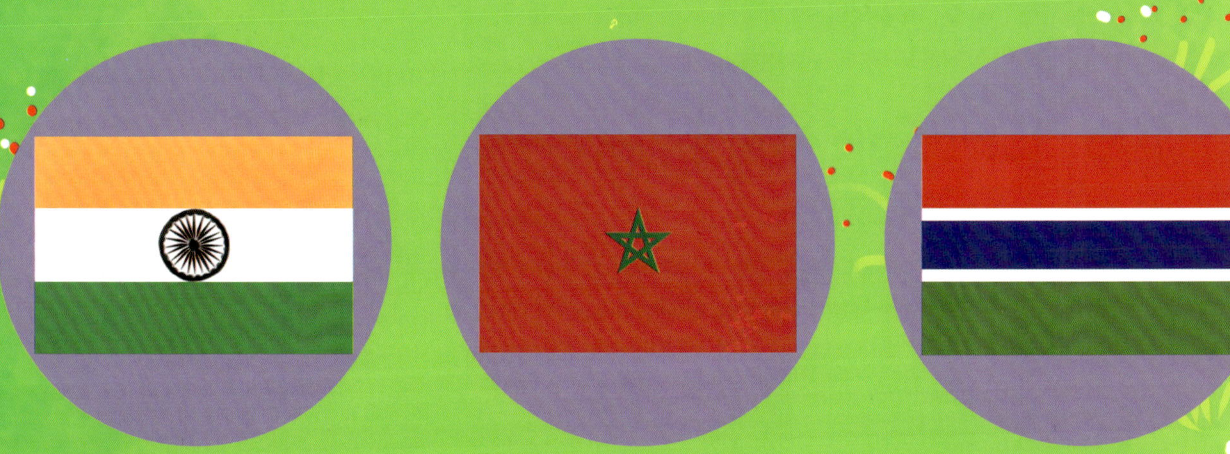

198. Morocco

Morocco plans to reduce its CO2 emissions to a level consistent with limiting warming to 1.5 degrees C. Morocco National Energy Strategy calls for generating 42% of its electricity production from renewables by 2020, and 52% by 2030. It has invested in the largest concentrated solar farm in the world, which covers an area the size of 3,500 football fields, and generates enough electricity to power two cities the size of Marrakesh.

199. Republic of The Gambia

The Republic of The Gambia is the other country in West Africa, with a 1.5 degrees C emissions reduction strategy. The Gambia's National Water and Electricity Company (NAWEC) has completed the preliminary phase of a tender for a 20 MW solar project in the Greater Banjul area in the west of the country.

The country has also launched a large project to restore 10,000 hectares of forests, mangroves, and savannas. It is also replacing flooded rice paddies with dry upland rice fields and is promoting the adoption of efficient cook stoves to reduce the overuse of forest resources.

200. India

India has emerged as a global leader in renewable energy, and in fact is investing more in renewable energy sources than in fossil fuels, having established a goal of generating 40% of its power through renewables by 2030.

201. Costa Rica

Costa Rica aims for its electricity production to be 100 percent renewable by 2021. It is very close to its target. In 2018, it generated 98% of its electricity primarily through hydropower. The country has made it a national priority to use renewable energy across its roads and rails. Additionally, in February 2019, Costa Rica banned oil extraction and exploitation from 2021 until the end of 2050.

202. Norway

Norway is showing signs of progress. It has set an ambitious target of reducing emissions by 40% by 2030 and it has adopted legislation committing the country to reduce emissions by 80% -95% relative to 1990 levels by 2050. Forest cover is increasing. And electricity production almost entirely comes from renewables- 96% from hydropower and 2% from wind farms.

203. Are Dams a Boon or a Bane?

Dams are more bane than boon. They do help to protect us from floods and prevent them by storing water. They are one of the major sources of harnessing renewable hydroelectricity. But their negative effects on the environment outweigh their positive effects. Massive dam construction often causes flooding of land, and thus destroys agricultural lands. Dams are often built in ecologically sensitive locations, which ultimately destroy the ecology and animal biodiversity of the place, as well as the river. Dams cause displacement of the original inhabitants of that place, rendering them homeless in some cases.

204. DIY (Do It Yourself): How to Purify Camp Water

Often on long camping trips, it is difficult to find clean water suitable for drinking and cooking. At the same time, carrying bottles of water is troublesome. But alum and bleaching powder in our backpacks will not add much weight or take space and can easily purify the muddiest of muddy water, making it suitable for drinking and cooking. Both alum which is the short form for Aluminium Sulphate, and bleaching powder or chlorinated lime, are commonly available in most grocery stores.

Alum treatment

1. Collect muddy water in a bucket. Remove any visible floating material by hand.
2. Use a fine cloth to filter out the floating and suspended macro particles along with some silt of the muddy water into another vessel.

3. About 10 - 15 mg of alum is required per litre of water. So in a bucket with five litres of water, add half a teaspoon of powdered alum. Stir well.

4. Keep the bucket still for about 6 to 7 hours so that the sediments get coagulated and settle down at the bottom.
5. After keeping it undisturbed for about seven hours, you may see most of the dissolved particles settled down at the bottom of the bucket. Decant the clean water into another vessel very slowly without disturbing the sediments, leaving about half a litre of water in the bucket with the sediments.

For clearer water, repeat the fine cloth filtration process.

Disinfection

6. Sedimentation cleans the water to some extent but it does not get rid of the bacteria. This is the task accomplished by chlorine in the bleach solution. The chlorination process kills almost 90% per cent of the bacteria present in water. For every one litre of water 2 drops of bleach solution are prescribed. Stir well and keep it for 30 minutes with intermittent stirring. So, for 4 litres of water add 9 drops of bleach solution. The water may smell a bit of chlorine, so keep it in the open.

Precautions

The bleaching solution is corrosive. Take care not to get your skin or cloth in contact with the solution.

4 litres of clean cooking and drinking water is available to you for camping.

205. Dead Sea Salt Soap

Chemical soaps are easily available and are made from oil, foaming materials, preservatives, and more. It's true that soap is washed up with water and does not remain on the skin, which reduces its influence, but it can cause unpleasant dryness and irritation as we have no idea of the chemicals used. Even if soap is biodegradable, it is not safe to put that soap directly into the water. All soap, whether biodegradable or not, contains chemicals that detrimentally affect lake chemistry. It can also harm fish and other aquatic organisms. Dead sea salt soap is one such soap produced from the Dead Sea minerals with a combination of natural oils and distilled water, essential oils for added effect, scent, and aroma. This natural soap acts as a purifier and does not pollute groundwater, unlike chemical soaps.

206. Turning Babies' Dirty Diapers into Fruit Trees

No, this is not a joke! This IS possible. The main condition is that one has to make sure that the babies' poop is disposed of only in compostable diapers. The used ones are then handed over to the collector, who processes and transforms these within approximately six months into hygienic black soil, high in organic compounds. Fruits and vegetables grown in this are much richer in vitamins and minerals. This practice has been adopted successfully by many who are committed to the cause of not polluting the environment and who follow the principle of a Blue Economy that guides us to simply use what we have, generate more value to it and be inspired by nature.

207. Diaper Waste into Fruit Trees

Let us learn about the basic steps on how to turn compostable diaper waste into fruit trees.

- Take a bucket and then layer it with biochar powder, along with any organic material—kitchen waste, coffee grinds, or used diapers—it's the same.
- Fill the bucket to the top and wait for four weeks. During this fermentation process, microorganisms multiply. Then it's time to bring in the worms.
- The fermented layers from the bucket are mixed with soil, making it aerobic.
- The microorganisms such as fungi and bacteria work intensively on organic materials. The worms, in turn, feed on the microorganisms—and will then produce six times more microorganisms in the final stage of black soil production, during worm composting. Microorganisms are essential for healthy soil.

208. Urban Heat Island Effect

It is a known fact that cities tend to get insufferably hotter, more so than surrounding rural areas. This is the urban heat island effect, in which pavements, buildings and roads readily absorb the sun's energy and release it well into the night. This effect increases energy costs (e.g., for air conditioning), air pollution levels, and heat-related illness and mortality. Whereas, tall trees and vegetation of rural areas, by contrast, provide shade and cool the air by releasing water. An international team of researchers has used a new modeling technique to estimate that by the year 2100, the world's cities could warm by as much as 4.4 degrees Celsius on average.

To reduce the urban heat island effect:

- Improve on green infrastructure.
- Plant trees and other vegetation.
- Build green roofs.
- Install cool roofs.
- Exercise traditional water quality practices by adding trees in or around roadside planters.
- Use green infiltration-based practices to boost roadside cooling and shading.
- Use energy-efficient appliances and equipment.

209. Heat & Humidity

Changing temperature and humidity are the two factors that are the conspiring menaces of extreme heat. Our bodies respond to high temperatures by perspiring, and as the sweat evaporates it cools the body. But humidity makes this process less efficient because the moisture in the air does not readily accept the evaporating sweat from our bodies. That's why humid heat feels so much more uncomfortable than dry heat. Humidity increases the risk of overheating and organ failure, since one can't sweat efficiently to cool down. Greening of the private and public spaces beautifies them, provides people with shade and also helps in reducing the heat. Each leaf on the tree acts like a tiny air conditioner, releasing moisture to cool the environment, thus reducing the menaces of extreme heat.

210. Solar-powered Mud House

The Indian armed forces stationed at 12,000 feet above sea-level in Ladakh lack access to 24×7 electricity. This lets them turn to other heating solutions like burning diesel, kerosene or firewood, which is not a very environmentally-friendly solution.

However, Sonam Wangchuk, an engineer, education reformist and environmentalist in Ladakh has found a solution by inventing a solar-powered mud house that not only emits less pollution but is also more efficient and a perfect solution to the cold for many soldiers who come from the warmer plains. He uses pre-fabricated bricks made from local materials like clay, fibre and waste to make solar heated mud huts that are eco-friendly and require little external heating.

These solar mud houses ensure that the temperature inside can remain 40 degrees higher than the outside temperature in peak winters. Say, the temperature outside is minus 20 degrees Celsius, it will be 20 degrees Celsius inside the hut, that too without using any heating appliances. These solar huts prevent pollution caused by the massive amounts of oil the army consumes to keep the jawans warm.

211. Ice Stupa

Ice Stupa is an artificial glacier grafting technique, used for storing winter water which otherwise causes runoff of unused water. The concept is very similar to making ice lollies from crushed ice. It is in the form of conical shaped ice heaps. During summer, when water is scarce, the Ice Stupa melts to increase the water supply for crops. Ice Stupa was also invented by the engineer, innovator and education reformist Sonam Wangchuk, who is the founder-director of the NGO Students' Educational and Cultural Movement of Ladakh (SECMOL). Sonam Wangchuk was awarded the Rolex Awards for Enterprise for his work on Ice Stupa.

212. Impact of Lost and Fragmented Habitat

Habitat loss is the leading cause of biodiversity loss worldwide. Animals, no matter how big or small, are all dependent on their habitat. They need a given amount of area to be able to find enough resources to maintain viable populations. But once the area of available habitat goes below a certain threshold, populations are no longer viable and species go locally extinct.

By understanding how habitat loss affects interactions between different species, in different environments, we should be concerned with not just the loss of a single species but rather the way those whole communities are affected by human-induced threats. We must adopt biodiversity strategies that need to take into account community interactions, as well as the shape of habitat loss, in order to better preserve future biodiversity.

213. 'Flying Dogs'

"Sharing is caring". This act of compassion to care for those in need has been such an integral part of our lives. Often leftovers are extended to our furry stray friends as they will eat anything when hungry. This is far better than discarding fairly good food into bins that later becomes a nuisance. Another way to extend this act of compassion is to include some of the feathered friends, especially the ones who vocalise their feelings in response to hunger or threat through their distinctive 'caw-caw' sound, crows, the "flying dogs". Their diet involves over a thousand different food items, from worms, insects, and carries on to scraps of food, bones, eggshells, fruits and seeds. So, those living in urban heights can opt for mutualism by welcoming the "Flying dogs" to help them tackle their food waste.

214. Scraps Trap Mosquitoes

Empty containers often become the breeding site for mosquitoes. What if this can be turned around with some modification and be used as mosquito traps!

All you need to make non-poisonous and eco-friendly homemade mosquito traps are household items that don't need to be dumped into the waste bins, like a used 1.5 - 2 L plastic bottle, old newspaper or opaque polybag, scissors or cutter, tape, sugar, preferably brown, and warm water. Take the help of an adult especially when handling sharp objects and scissors.

Step 1.	• Cut the top of a 1.5L bottle, using scissors or a cutter. • Remove the cap and recycle.
Step 2.	• In 200ml of warm water, add 50g of sugar. • Dissolve the sugar and pour this into the bottle.
Step 3.	• Once cool, add 1g of yeast into the sugar solution. • Stirring is not required. • The sugar feeds the yeast, which then releases carbon dioxide, which attracts mosquitoes.
Step 4.	• Invert the bottle top into the cut bottom. • Keep enough room between the funnel and the liquid for the mosquito to fly around.
Step 5.	• Wrap and tape the plastic bottle with a used newspaper or an opaque polybag.

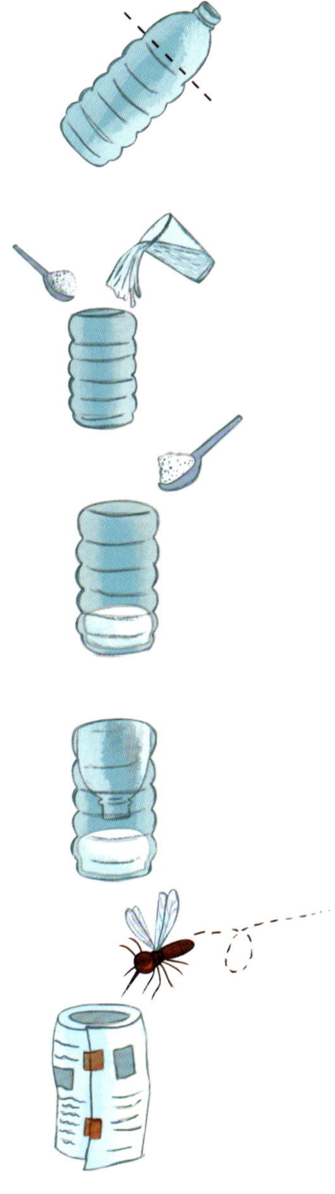

215. Build a Carbon Sink Pond in Your Own Backyard

A pond is a biodiversity hotspot much richer in species compared to rivers, streams and lakes. Globally, ponds may also be important in influencing atmospheric carbon by storing and releasing it.

When deciding on the type of pond that would be most appropriate for your space, it may be beneficial to spend some time researching the options. But once you're done, follow the below steps on how to build your pond.

Some of the things to consider before you start digging that hole or building the space are:

Step 1 – Appropriate location

Remember that any overhanging trees, even evergreens, are going to drop leaves into the water that will need cleaning of the pond frequently to protect its ecology.

Also, avoid locations where runoff from rain will flow into the pond. It will be difficult to control the flow of dirt, fertiliser and other debris into the pond. These water run-offs can damage the environment and kill the fish and plants living in it.

Step 2 – Pick a size according to the available space

'Cut your coat according to your cloth' is a popular saying which means to make plans and decisions that are based on what you have and not what you would like. Similarly, the size you choose will depend on the space available to you, and the amount of money that is in your budget for building the pond.

Step 3 – Dig or build, your take

Your pond can be as small as 3-4 feet in diameter and about 2 feet deep. If you plan to keep some plants near the pond, dig a shelf around its perimeter that's about one foot deep and 1-2 feet wide.

Step 4 – Line the pond

Waterproofing is essential, so, line the hole with suitable waterproof material and ensure it is leak-proof.

Step 5 – Filter or fountain, it depends!

Filters are not essential for a pond with no fish. But if you do use one, a filter will keep your fish healthy, as it keeps circulating the water and oxygenates it, thus preventing any bad odours and much more.

Solar Pond Pumps are often used as environmentally friendly solutions for constant water flow around a pond, thereby also saving the pond owner from electrical bills, as SOLAR ENERGY is FREE!

Step 6 – Fill the pond with water

Use clean water to fill the pond especially if you plan to keep fish. De-chlorinate the water and just let your new pond sit for about a week before adding fish or plants so that the chlorine in the water would have evaporated.

Step 7 – Add your aquatic flora and fauna

Choose appropriate material which will not contaminate the water and decorate the pond as you like with stones, pebbles, colourful aquatic plants and fish.

Fresh water fish add colour, beauty and vitality to your pond. The brilliantly coloured fish in the shades of gold, yellow and white are a breath-taking contrast to the deep greens of plants and the dark water of the pond.

Take experts' opinions and do your homework on the species that are well suited to the type of pond you have built, the ecosystem available to them and even the number of fish, as they will grow to fit the size of the pond. So even if you choose a regular size goldfish, it will eventually grow bigger than what you'd normally expect from a small aquarium.

216. Tyre Pond

Disposal of waste tyres is a challenging task because tyres have a long life and are non-biodegradable. The traditional methods of disposal of waste tyres have been stockpiling, illegal dumping or landfilling, all of which are short-term solutions.

So, let us learn the steps for making a tyre pond in your backyard instead, to give it a second life.

217. Colour-coded

Biomedical waste or hospital waste is any kind of waste containing infectious (or potentially infectious) materials. Disposal of this waste is an environmental concern, as many medical wastes are classified as infectious or biohazardous and could potentially lead to the spread of infectious diseases. The latest guidelines for segregation of bio-medical waste recommend the following colour-coding for safe and secure disposal:

Red Bag – Syringes (without needles), soiled gloves, catheters, IV tubes, etc., should all be disposed of in a red-coloured bag, which will later be incinerated.

Yellow Bag – All dressings, bandages and cotton swabs with body fluids, blood bags, human anatomical waste, body parts are to be discarded in yellow bags.

Cardboard box with blue marking – Glass vials, ampules, other glassware is to be discarded in a cardboard box with a blue marking/sticker.

White Puncture Proof Container (PPC) – Needles, sharps, blades are disposed of in a white, translucent, puncture-proof container.

Black Bags – These are to be used for non-biomedical waste. In a hospital setup, this includes stationery, vegetable and fruit peels, leftovers, packaging including that from medicines, disposable caps, disposable masks, disposable shoe-covers, disposable teacups, cartons, sweeping dust, kitchen waste, etc.

218. Packet Food

To maintain optimum health, it is necessary to pay special attention to our everyday diet.

But today we are busier than ever and it is a struggle to make nutritious meals and snacks a part of our regular diet. And that is how we fall prey to easily available processed and packaged food.

Food processing removes essential nutrients, vitamins and fibre present in the food. Processed food has a longer shelf life but loses nutritional value. The food may become tastier because of the added fats, sugar, salt and artificial chemicals for preserving, colouring and flavouring. However, all these are associated with major health risks: excess salt can increase blood pressure, excess sugar can cause weight gain and excess fats can increase cholesterol levels. Chemicals rarely add to the nutritional value but are believed to be cancer-causing agents, thus adding to health risks.

On the other hand, eating fresh food will help you live a long and healthy life, as the nutritional value of all its ingredients is intact. Cooking your food or purchasing and eating freshly-made food is the best way to ensure no preservatives, additives, chemicals, or colours have been added to it. Freshly prepared food loses its nutritional value over time, so the quicker it's eaten, the more nutrients you gain from it.

Choose food that heals your body. Eat wisely and stay healthy.

219. Minimising Carbon Footprint

Our carbon footprint measures the total amount of greenhouse gases emitted as a result of our daily activities. Here are some ways that will help minimise our carbon footprint:

1. Avoid air conditioner overuse.

2. Avoid water heater overuse. Turn it off.

3. Spend time in as much natural light as possible. Natural light helps people to be happier, healthier, calmer and more productive.

4. Reduce travel by car or air to maintain smaller carbon footprints.

5. Make the most of video conferencing. Travel only if you must.

6. Unplug/switch off devices rather than leaving them on stand-by/ hibernate.

7. Gift a plant for life. Flowers stay only for a few days or less.

8. Recycle to the extent practical and possible.

9. Avoid wasting water. Every drop counts.

10. Avoid bottled water. Plastics are neurotoxic.

11. Put in insulation wherever needed to increase efficiency, and switch to CFL (/LED).

12. Increase efforts towards adding greenery wherever possible.

220. Benefits of Natural Light

People subconsciously seek out sunlit places and enjoy spending time in natural light.

Here are some of the benefits of natural lighting on our health, well-being, wallet and the environment as a whole.

Natural lighting reduces eye strain and makes it easier for people to see.

It prevents depression in adults as well as in children and boosts one's spirits.

Vitamin D is an essential mineral for all people and has numerous health benefits. Exposure to sunlight is the primary method through which people receive a sufficient amount of vitamin D.

A well-ventilated sunlit house is significantly free from mildew and mould growth. Sunlight keeps the space cleaner and healthier for you and your family.

221. REUSING a Plastic Bottle

Here is a handy tip for removing a broken light bulb:

1. Turn off the power before removing a broken bulb that is still stuck in the bulb socket.
2. Take an empty plastic water bottle and slowly heat the mouth with a candle, just enough to soften the plastic and make it sticky.
3. Press the bottle mouth into the broken bulb's base, which is slightly larger. Hold the bottle still for a few seconds, allowing it to cool and stick to the base of the broken bulb.
4. While maintaining slight pressure, slowly turn the bottle counterclockwise to unscrew the bulb's base until it is clear of the socket.

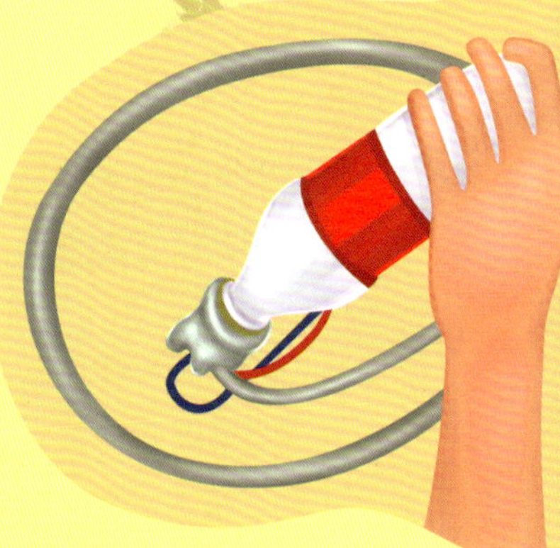

DO NOT TRY THIS WITHOUT ADULT SUPERVISION

222. Bamboo Can Fight Climate Change

Nearly 10% of Malawi's (a country in southeastern Africa) forests have disappeared since 2001 due to uncontrolled clearing of native trees, to grow crops. This is because around 80% of Malawians rely on agriculture for their livelihoods. Almost 96% of Malawi's rapidly growing population depends on wood or charcoal for cooking. As in other countries in sub-Saharan Africa, these two factors put pressure on forests, increasing climate-warming emissions, disrupting groundwater and reducing biodiversity.

The country has committed to restoring 11 million acres of degraded land by 2030, by planting bamboo to fight climate change and restore the forest. Other countries like Kenya are already using bamboo, as it grows incredibly quickly, taking a few years to mature. It can be harvested again and again in its 80 years of lifespan.

The advantage of bamboo is that it is a quick and effective substitute for trees, it thickens the forest, regrows quickly when cut down, stops landslides and absorbs carbon dioxide and other greenhouse gases quite efficiently.

Could planting more bamboo help our forests too?

223. Mixed Forests vs. Monoculture Forests

Besides timber and other commercial production, a forest contributes to ecosystem services such as biological diversity in flora and fauna, carbon storage and food. Studies have shown that mixed forests, in comparison with forests having the same type of plants (monoculture) have positive effects on several different areas, including production.

- High diversity of tree species has a favourable impact on processes in the ecosystem.
- Studies show that the role played by the growth of diverse tree species includes six different ecosystem services, that is tree growth, carbon storage, berry production, food for wildlife, the existence of dead wood, and biological diversity which is positively related to the number of tree species.

Both forestry and nature conservation stand to gain by promoting a greater variety of tree types, thereby providing more diverse ecosystem services.

224. ZBNF

Zero-Budget Natural Farming (ZBNF) is a radical indigenous farming technique gaining mass acceptance in some parts of India as it follows the principle of 'Back to Basics'. It is a climate-resilient, low-cost, natural sustainable agricultural practice. It utilises locally-sourced resources such as indigenous cow dung-urine and locally available plant organic matter. It totally avoids the use of inorganic fertilisers and pesticides. This practice is not only environment-friendly but also cost-effective, owing primarily to the use of easily available low-cost farm inputs.

225. Permaculture

Permaculture, i.e., 'permanent agriculture', is defined as 'a philosophy of working with nature, rather than against it; and of looking at plants and animals in all their functions, instead of treating any area as a single product system'.

For example, roofs are used to catch the water that can be used in the kitchen. From there, it drains into grey water irrigation systems. These feed the plants, which in turn provide food and fuel (wood). Each of these elements is then put back into the system as compost. No waste is created. No resources are imported.

The following examples of permaculture gardening techniques can help to establish sustainable soils that will make your fruits and vegetables grow as sustainably and as nutritious as possible:

No-dig gardening

1. Keyhole garden designs
2. Worm composting
3. Chop-and-drop organic mulch
4. Companion gardening
5. Rotational cropping and
6. Green manure

226. Making Vegans Happy

Vegans miss out on certain animal food like honey, milk and milk products, because they strongly believe that all creatures have the right to life and freedom. They oppose ending a conscious being's life simply to consume its flesh, drink its milk, or wear its skin — especially because alternatives are available.

Now scientists have found a solution to change all this by making honey without bees, milk without cows and eggs without chicken. Many start-up companies are now using the fermentation process to produce vegan products that are identical biologically to the real thing. By tailoring the micro-organism carefully and choosing the right feedstocks, it's possible to create a different end product - anything from honey, to egg whites and milk. Fermentation technology allows controlling, and the results even surpass the texture, taste and culinary functionality of animal-derived egg counterparts. They create a type of honey, identical to the natural kind in every molecule, but produced without involving any bees at all, leaving them to prosper and thrive in the wild.

227. Bring the BEES Back

A single honeybee typically visits around 7,000 flowers a day, and it takes four million flower visits to produce a kilogram of honey. Globally, 81 million hives produce 1.6 million tonnes of honey.

The world has lost nearly 40% of the honeybee population. Honeybees are the most famous of the pollinators, and account for over a third of global food crop production. Their absence would remove a host of nutritious foods from our diets, including potatoes, onions, strawberries, cauliflower, pepper, coffee, pumpkins, carrots, sunflowers, apples, almonds, tomatoes and cocoa, etc. The declining bee population will adversely affect our food security besides causing danger to biodiversity.

So the wise thing to do is to bring the bees back by planting more fruit trees, maintaining gardens with a variety of flower-bearing plants and starting a kitchen garden in your backyard.

228. No-dig Gardening

Soil is not just 'dirt' to anchor plant and tree roots, though that's how many people treat it. Soil is a very complex ecosystem, teeming with very diverse life-forms. When we dig or till, we kill beneficial bacteria, organisms, and creatures and when there's no soil life left to decompose, the result will be nutrient-deficient soils. Therefore, we should try to encourage soil life rather than deplete it.

No-dig gardening is a widely used technique designed to preserve the soil life that converts organic matter into plant food. The beds are built on top of existing soil, which has several benefits. Apart from saving soil organisms, it provides a double dose of quality soil.

In humid climates, no-dig beds help to make sure that water drains the soil well. The use of deep mulches ensures that the soils stay sufficiently moist, cutting down on maintenance and water use.

229. Root Them Back

The incidents of cyclones have increased due to global warming. This results in severe destruction of life and property. One such consequence is the uprooting of thousands of trees. As it is, we are losing trees in large numbers in the name of development. Do you know you can give a second life to an uprooted tree by just jacking it upright and rooting it back to the soil, where it got pulled out in the first place? Give it a try! You never know, it may start bearing fruits again, all thanks to the effort you put in.

230. Worm Composting

Composting with worms (also known as vermicomposting) is a great way to save the environment. It provides a convenient method to dispose of organic waste, such as vegetable peelings. It saves space in the landfill, which is good for the environment, gives worms a happy home and all the free 'eats' that they could want. For those who have gardens or even potted plants, home-grown compost is a great way to feed and nurture plants.

Vermi-compost is the product of this composting process using various species of worms, usually red wigglers, white worms, and other earthworms to create a mixture of decomposing vegetable or food waste and bedding materials.

The worms break down the kitchen scraps into worm castings that are much more fertile than typical compost. This gardening technique works well with both raised beds and keyhole designs.

Simply drill a bunch of nickel-sized holes into the bottom half of a 5-gallon bucket. Then bury the bucket in the garden, with the bottom half beneath the soil surface.

Fill the bucket with a bed of shredded paper and/or cardboard topped off with a layer of soil, manure and/or dried grass. The worms will handle the rest. The nutrients of the vermicompost drain directly into the garden and feed the plants. When the bucket is full, the castings can be spread over the bed.

231. Chop-and-drop Organic Mulch

Nitrogen-fixing plants harvest their nitrogen from the air and store it in nodules of their roots. When a plant is pruned above the ground, it mimics the action below the surface. In this case, it leads to a boost in fertilisation of the soil from the mulch and also below in the roots.

This technique doubles up on the benefits, especially for organic mulch, with a wide range of benefits.

- It moderates soil temperature by keeping the direct sunlight away and insulating it from the cold.
- It prevents evaporation so that the soil stays moist.
- It stops heavy rains and wind from eroding the topsoil.
- As it breaks down, it enriches the soil with more organic matter to feed on.

232. Seed Paper

Seed paper is produced by mixing the recycled paper pulp with seeds and pressing the mixture into a shape. This can be used for any type of used paper like plain white paper, glossy paper, newspaper, tissue paper, cardboard, etc., to create the pulp. Tear, soak, blend and lift paper mixed with seeds. Use seeds that are tiny so that the result is a textured paper with a more natural look than store-bought options. Seed paper can even be planted in soil where the seeds should grow if the soil is kept moist. Seed paper is excellent to use for gift tags and cards. Do write a note on the seed paper to inform the recipient that they can plant the paper, and tell them which seeds you used.

233. Fair Share

Gardening centres on three core ethics: Earth care, people care, and fair share. In terms of gardening, 'fair share' means that we can't constantly take from our gardens without giving back.

Green manure is a way to give back to the garden. This process involves growing a veggie patch or forest garden, to replenish or build soils with minimal input. Owing to nature and photosynthesis, the green manure plants convert sunlight into biomass and nutrients for us, for free.

Natural systems work this way: Things grow, die, and go back to the Earth so that the next generation can benefit from them. If we only harvest from our annual gardens, the soil never gets back the energy lost in producing those crops.

It's only fair to our soil to occasionally grow something. Many gardeners grow green manure as part of the crop rotation.

234. Vegan Leather

Two entrepreneurs from Mexico have created vegan leather out of the cactus leaves of the Prickly Pear. The cruelty-free leather is called Desserto.

The vegan leather is partially biodegradable. Its texture is like regular leather. It is flexible, breathable, and lasts for at least 10 years and is free of toxic chemicals that are used to treat regular leather. It can replace the use of regular leather and save animals from slaughterhouses. It can be used in furniture, cars, leather accessories, clothing, etc.

Next time you buy a belt or a bag, check out if it is vegan!

235. Birds Can Buy Happiness

A new study suggests that high biological diversity, especially of birds, can increase life satisfaction and can buy happiness, just as much as money can. During the COVID-19 pandemic, nature has emerged as an escape from quarantine and social isolation. The social isolation necessitated by the Coronavirus pandemic has pushed many people to escape into the outdoors and reconnect with nature. Research suggests that spending more time in nature and experiencing numerous different bird species in their daily life, can help people relax and reduce physical and mental stress.

Climate change, however, is threatening many species' habitats. This poses a risk to human well-being as well. Conserving nature, therefore, constitutes an investment in the well-being of all human beings.

236. INNOVATIVE IDEAS

Biodegradable Lunch Box

Does a zero-waste, 100% biodegradable and plastic-free lunch box as tough as a Tupperware sound too good to you?

Organic rice husk with a natural binding agent found in plants is used to make the box. The manufacturer claims the lunch box is durable, greaseproof and leak-proof, oven and microwave safe and can even survive in the dishwasher and the freezer.

When discarded into a landfill, the lunch box will biodegrade within 180 days. Next time you go to buy a lunch box go for something that is biodegradable or lasts forever. Even better!

237. Never-ending Notebook

A company has come up with a notebook the pages of which can be wiped clean with a damp cloth after writing.

This never-ending notebook could save a lot of trees over a lifetime for sure. The concept is very similar to the magical erasable slates kids use to learn to draw and write on. You can make one for yourself using a used plastic sheet, cardboard, paper and glue.

238. Coding

Coding can help preserve nature and biodiversity.

Since 1974, the world has celebrated Environment Day every year on 5 June, but issues like air pollution, water contamination, deforestation, endangered wildlife have not been solved. In fact, we are witnessing the impact of these degradations daily in our lives. A conscious improvement in our habits and behaviours can make a positive change. Computer science enables researchers and scientists to use large-scale data to investigate and analyse issues like climate change and water contamination. Google initiated a new program called Made with Code where girls can code their own environmental awareness statement and share it on social media. This program showed that conversations around science, technology, engineering and mathematics can come together to find alternative solutions to environmental challenges.

239. The Internet

Technology allows us to work remotely which can reduce air pollution in cities. Especially during a pandemic, video conference programs reduce the need to commute for meetings, resulting in decreased fuel consumption, which in turn means cleaner air. People print less and opt for communication through email and messenger services.

240. Ocean Pollution

Plastic pollution in the oceans has been a critical topic for years and the problem has become severe. Initiatives like Plastic Adrift have been able to create statistical models to track the paths of these isles of plastic trash and eventually identify their source.

Projects like these help kids to raise awareness and instil a responsible lifestyle within themselves.

241. Freshwater Supply

Freshwater is an invaluable but scarce resource, especially in some parts of the world. UN Environment, Google and the European Commission have launched a data platform to track the world's water bodies. The app enables all countries to monitor their freshwater supply. Search for it and explore!

242. Forest Health

As long as forests exist there is hope for fresh air. However, forests are threatened by many factors like climate change, drought, rising temperatures and above all the human factor. That's why scientists use geographic information systems to collect and analyse relevant data to help preserve forests.

243. Wildlife Corridors

Planet Earth's size is not increasing but the human population is, leaving very little space for wild animals that also share this planet. A way to reduce the impact of urbanisation is to create wildlife corridors – areas of protected land where animals are safe. Scientists are compiling massive amounts of data to create models of the areas inhabited by wildlife. This way, by applying a computational approach, they can predict the location of animals and design the corridors accordingly.

244. Protecting Habitats

When large forest areas are cleared to develop human infrastructure, the forest patches which are left are often not enough to support larger populations. That's where remote sensing technologies come into play to enable the use of information, collected by satellites, to monitor animals and protect their habitats and learn about biodiversity in the process.

245. How Food Is Refined

Making a smart choice will not only benefit our health but also reduce our carbon footprint. Remember, the more processing a food item goes through, the higher the carbon emission.

246. Celtic Sea Salt vs. Refined Salt

Salt in its natural form is unrefined and not altered by humans. It contains many different elements that are essential for our body.

Celtic sea salt contains 80 natural minerals and elements required for life compared to the refined salt most commonly used by all with only two major items: Sodium and Chloride.

The commercial salt is refined with chemicals to remove minerals as they are referred to as 'impurities'. The chemicals used to treat refined salt can include sulphuric acid and chlorine. It is this chemical treatment of refined salt, which causes acidosis (lowered pH). Our bodies were meant to function optimally with adequate mineral levels and adequate salt intake. Only the use of unrefined salt can provide both of these factors.

247. Sugar

Both refined sugar and jaggery are obtained from the same source, sugarcane. However, they both have huge differences in terms of their properties and benefits as they are treated and processed differently.

Refined sugar contains no nutrients, just calories with chemicals added to it during the refining process. It breaks down immediately, causing insulin and blood sugar levels to skyrocket. One doesn't feel full regardless of how many calories one consumes. All the unburnt energy is stored as fat and might lead to obesity.

Whole forms of sugar, such as fruit, are ideal because of the fibre and lower calorie content, which will leave you feeling satisfied a lot faster. If you really want some cane sugar, chew on sugarcane!

Raw, unrefined sugar actually has some nutrients and this is why foods like honey, brown rice syrup, maple sugar, cane juice, date sugar, fruit and molasses are better for our health. In fact, original sugar cane has 10-15% of sugar concentration and the rest of it is water, fibre, enzyme, vitamin, and minerals. Refined sugar has 99.5% sucrose and 0.5% water.

248. Oil

Unrefined oil is the oil that has been processed with minimal to no heat. It is usually referred to as cold pressed or expeller pressed oil. Oils that you find labelled as raw, pure, virgin are all unrefined oils. These oils are the best oils for topical use as well as consumption.

Refined oils, on the other hand, have been bleached or deodorised to extract the maximum amount of oil. This process reduces the nutrients in the oil and compromises its effectiveness. If you can find the unrefined version of oil, it is the best version.

249. Homemade Soaps to Fight Malaria

Malaria continues to be a killer disease. Malaria represents up to 40 per cent of hospital admissions and more than 4 per cent of the public health expenditure in most countries in the African continent. Preventive measures like mosquito nets and vaccination are still out of reach for a majority of Africans. But amidst these grim statistics lies hope in a low-cost soap.

Gerard Niyondiko, a chemical graduate from the University of Burundi, has come up with a locally-made soap that promises to make malaria a thing of the past.

Joan Nalubega, a woman in Uganda, has also been fighting malaria with homemade soaps. She was inspired to do this by her personal experience. As a child, she was frequently ill from malaria, which motivated her to tackle Uganda's number one infectious disease through a long-lasting mosquito-repellent soap.

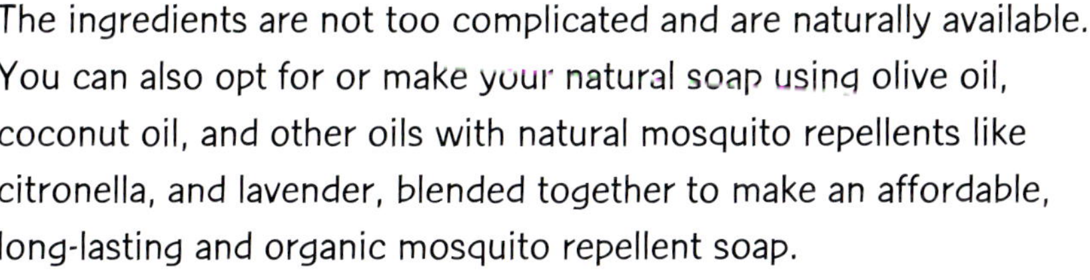

A mosquito-repellent soap offers a new way to offer protection against malaria. An affordable and accessible repellent solution that will save people who are unwilling or unable to spend more to protect themselves against the deadly disease. It would integrate malaria prevention into the everyday life of the population without any change of habits. The soap can be found even in the most remote areas in Africa, even in conflict zones, where intervention against malaria is impossible.

The ingredients are not too complicated and are naturally available. You can also opt for or make your natural soap using olive oil, coconut oil, and other oils with natural mosquito repellents like citronella, and lavender, blended together to make an affordable, long-lasting and organic mosquito repellent soap.

250. If You Care for Yourself....

Standing up for the environment is one of the most important, rewarding things you can do right now. Our Earth needs more protection than ever before. Caring about the environment can be exhausting, and to do so, self-care is equally essential. Self-care isn't a self-indulgent privilege; it is practical and important. It plays an integral role in our ability to continue to support the cause of taking care of the environment. So, take note and listen to your mind and body.

Sleep for 8 hours a night, your brain needs it. But blue light from appliances messes with your body's ability to prepare for sleep. It blocks a hormone called melatonin that makes you sleepy. So, switch OFF the mains before you sleep. It also saves idle energy.

Relax your eyes by massaging your feet with oil before bed. Use any cold pressed oil that is free of any kind of energy consuming processing, or is not loaded with all sorts of chemicals that may not be environment-friendly.

Avoid cold foods to care for your stomach. They are harder to digest and can negatively impact the immune system. Refrigeration consumes energy, which raises CO2 emission and contributes to global warming.

Avoiding excess fatty food will take care of your liver. But never pour used cooking oil down the drain! A single litre of waste cooking oil can pollute a million litres of water.

Replacing junk food with vegetables will take care of your intestines and the environment at the same time, as it grossly reduces one's carbon footprint.

Drink lots of water during the day for healthy kidneys. But remember the source is our rivers so increase your **HANDPRINT** by taking appropriate and responsible action to save the rivers from pollution.

Take care of your kidneys. Empty your bladder before bed. A plastic bottle filled with water can be placed in the toilet tank to reduce the amount of water used per flush. To check for a toilet leak, place dye or food colouring into the tank. Save every drop!

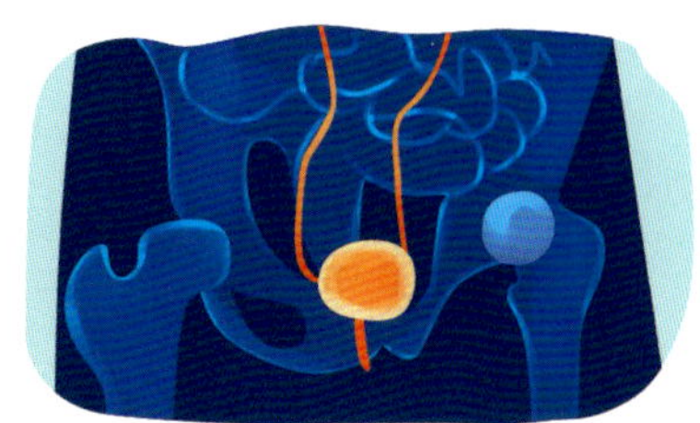

Eating raw onion regularly will take care of the urinary tract.

Food not only has a water footprint but also a carbon footprint. Onions have a low carbon footprint.

Regular consumption of green grams takes care of protein and iron deficiency and is beneficial for mensuration. Green gram grown by conventional agricultural processes causes increased greenhouse gas emissions, soil erosion, water pollution, and threatens human health. On the other hand, organically grown green gram has a smaller carbon footprint, conserves and builds soil health, replenishes natural ecosystems for cleaner water and air, all without toxic pesticide residues.

Care for your appendix, use lemon juice regularly. Lemons are loaded with beneficial nutrients. Having a lemon tree will thus contribute positively to the environmental eco-system of your home, giving you a beautiful and healthy garden!

Regular intake of pepper takes care of the throat. Sometimes unscrupulous people add mineral oil to peppercorns to act as a fungicide and to give a shiny look to peppercorns. The addition of mineral oil makes pepper unfit for human consumption. By simply stirring the peppercorns in water in the presence of an oily film or tiny oil droplets, the pepper is adulterated.

Avoid excess salt to take care of your heart. New research shows that there are microplastics in 90 percent of the table salt brands sampled worldwide. What we throw as trash, will come around someday!

251. This Mushroom Eats Plastic

Nature proves to be a problem-solver once again: In 2012, students at Yale University found that a rare species of mushroom from the Amazon rainforest is capable of subsisting on plastic alone. More precisely, Pestalotiopsis Microspora consumes polyurethane, the key ingredient in plastic products and converts it to organic matter.

The list of benefits of these mushrooms continues:

- Pestalotiopsis Microspora can live without oxygen, which suggests enormous potential for feeding on, and thus cleaning up, landfills.
- Some plastic-eating species can be eaten themselves. Some mushrooms not only help break down plastic, but their finished products can also be used to create furniture and building materials and made into mushroom bricks.
- Mushrooms not only have the ability to remove pollutants from the soil but also enable the conversion of waste into biofuels.

252. Mushroom Bricks: Hopeful Future!

Fungi have dominated the world's undergrowth for millions of years. Their unique ability to decompose organic matter enables them to thrive on the life of other organisms. Over decades of research and development, scientists discovered technologies which allow engineers to use fungus as the main building material in future by creating mushroom bricks.

These are a wood particle mixture that has been inoculated with mycelium, which is the thread-like root structure of a mushroom. Mycelium acts as a natural 'glue' that forms a web-like mesh all around the particles, binding it all together and making these bricks durable.

It only takes five days for the mushrooms to transform organic matter into a viable brick, making the process cheap and efficient. Although it is not the same as conventional building materials, the early stages of mycelium material engineering are proving to be hopeful.

253. All It Needs Is the Right Attitude!

The Citarum River is the longest and largest river in West Java, Indonesia.

It is a mixture of toxic and hazardous chemicals from 2,800 factories, mainly textiles, that dump 280m tonnes of industrial waste daily into this river, creating an overwhelming stench with mercury and lead. The river also has a high level of deadly E-coli dumped by human and animal faeces!

Mountains of plastic waste and Styrofoam banks on either side are an eyesore from a distance. Making matters worse, many locals think nothing of tossing their household waste into its toxic waters, thus adding to the disaster zone. This poses a serious health risk, especially for the five million people living in the river's basin, who suffer from skin diseases like scabies and dermatitis, as well as respiratory infections from inhaling factory pollution. Using this polluted water is a risky calculation for many of the 38 million people who rely on it for irrigation, washing and even drinking the water from the world's number one dirtiest river.

Jakarta has a seemingly impossible goal now, and that is to make the Citarum water drinkable by 2025. Indonesia has vowed to clean up its act, along with stakeholders, government officials and thousands of soldiers.

254. Sharing Home with the Chirpy House Sparrow

The house sparrow is one of the most commonly found social bird species in urban as well as in rural areas in India. The birds are often found in groups of eight to ten, have learned to live in close contact with humans and have coexisted peacefully with humans for years. But the last two decades have seen a steep decline in their population and they are facing an uncertain future. Their population is believed to be declining for various reasons, ranging from the destruction of habitat to lack of insects for the young to thrive on, due to indiscriminate use of chemical pesticides. The construction of tall, fancy flat-reflecting glass panes, means that they offer no space for the birds to build their nests in the crevasses as they could in older buildings. They are also affected by radiation emitting from phone towers. Their decline means a bleak future for farms and farmers to do natural pest control.

But there is hope. 65 households at Borbali Samua, a little village in the Lakhimpur district of Assam, have joined hands to change all this. They have geared their homes and adopted the birds by sharing their home space with the chirpy house sparrows.

Jayanta Neog, the 47-year-old owner of a rice mill, is one of the principal conservators of the sparrow in this village. He goes around the village, educating adults and children about the importance of the sparrow. He makes artificial bird nests, using cardboard boxes, wooden boxes, shoeboxes and even bamboo. The sparrow easily adapts to manmade nests and if they are promoted on a large-scale, can lead to a long-term conservation of the bird. It is the need of the hour to start habitat conservation drives by switching to organic gardening, planting hedges and putting up artificial nest boxes dedicated to house sparrows.

255. Watermelons Gone Small

This is an interesting story told by an engineer from Goa about Parra, the village he used to live in. It shows how our environment has to be nurtured properly or else the impacts are devastating. "I am from the village of Parra in Goa, hence we are called Parrikars. My village is famous for its watermelons. When I was a child, the farmers would organise a watermelon-eating contest at the end of the harvest season in May. All the kids would be invited to eat as many watermelons as they wanted. Years later, I went to IIT Mumbai to study engineering. I went back to my village after 6.5 years. I went to the market looking for watermelons. They were all gone. The ones that were there were so small.

I went to see the farmer who hosted the watermelon-eating contest. His son had taken over. He would host the contest but there was a difference. When the older farmer gave us watermelons to eat, he would ask us to spit out the seeds into a bowl. We were told not to bite into the seeds. He was collecting the seeds for his next crop. We were unpaid child labourers, actually. He kept his best watermelons for the contest and he got the best seeds, which would yield even bigger watermelons the next year. His son, when he took over, realised that the larger watermelons would fetch more money in the market, so he sold the larger ones and kept the smaller ones for the contest. The next year, the watermelons were smaller, the year later even smaller. In watermelons, the generation is one year.

In seven years, Parra's best watermelons were finished."

256. The Picture Says It All....

We can reuse old, used plastic bottles to create canopies and sun shelter in place of wood and metal sheets which one obtains by deforestation and mining.

257. This Says It All.....

258. Day Zero

Cape Town became the world's first major city to look like it was about to run out of water due to climate change. Residents started showering standing over buckets to catch and re-use that water, recycling washing machine water, and limiting loo flushes to once a day and having only night-time irrigation. The government took an unprecedented gamble. They announced 'day zero' – a moment when dam levels would be so low that they would turn off the taps in Cape Town and send people to communal water collection points.

The following year, both human efforts and good rain played a significant role to delay day zero. City authorities constantly warn the residents that if more severe restrictions aren't adhered to, the pushed day zero could soon become a definite date again!

As global temperatures continue to rise, cities around the world need to realise that what happened in Cape Town could happen to any city, sooner or later. They will have to figure out how to do more with less water.

No water also means no life!

So, let's conserve and recycle the priceless resource. It is our duty to use every drop of water judiciously and recharge our depleting ground water table with every drop of rain water falling on our rooftop. Let us all take a pledge to save and conserve water.

Remember the day zero is not over, it is delayed!

259. Some Herbs and Vegetables You Can Grow Easily in Water

Peppermint: Growing peppermint in water is easy; just put fresh cuttings in water to grow new plants.

Oregano: Take cuttings of fresh growth and pot them in water. Start pinching the growing tips as soon as the plant starts to grow well.

Stevia: This sweet plant is good to have in the house to add to freshly brewed teas and beverages. Take cuttings of growing soft branches and place them in water. Provide a warm place and as much light as possible to keep this tropical plant happy and full of sweetness.

Lettuce: The easiest way to grow them hydroponically is to cut a stem and insert it in an inch of water in a cup.

Vegetables: The simple technique used to grow lettuce can be applied to grow many vegetables in water.

260. Vegetables and Plants Which Can Be Grown in Water

There are many ways to grow vegetables without needing a lot of space. Growing vegetables in water is one of them.

Follow the dos and don'ts and soon you can become an expert in growing herbs and vegetables in water using fresh cuttings. Do give it a try but don't give up!

- Avoid using chlorinated water directly as the bleaching chemical is not exactly friendly to plant tissues. Leave the tap water to air overnight, it dechlorinates the water. Spring water or well water are the best because they have some amount of dissolved minerals that may be of use to plants.

- Any container will do, glass or plastic, but coloured bottles are best, as roots generally like to grow away from light. So, one can just wrap a piece of paper around the bottle to keep the root zone in the dark. This will prevent algal growth on the container walls and on the root surface, which makes the bottles look untidy.

- Narrow-mouthed containers support the cuttings and keep them nearly upright, but not too narrow as the mouth of the container should allow free movement of air for the roots to breathe. If it has a wide mouth, then make sure there is proper netting. This will prevent mosquitoes from breeding.

- Soft cuttings are pretty quick to root in water. You don't need to use any rooting hormones. Just snip off 6-inch sections from growing tips and put them in the water-filled containers. Use the ones you get from the supermarket. Just wash them in plain water and cut off the lower portion.
- Remove lower leaves from cuttings and trim the lower tips close to the nodes from where the roots arise. When they are inserted into the bottles, there shouldn't be any leaves touching the water. They can rot easily and spoil the water, as they do in flower vases.
- Woody cuttings like rosemary may take longer to root, so be patient. Change the water once a week without disturbing the cuttings. Once the roots start to grow, usually between 2-6 weeks, water changes may not be necessary.

261. Self-powered Man

Mr Suresh, a graduate from IIT-Madras and IIM-Ahmedabad, has a huge canopy and an array of bamboo trees and climbers in his Chennai house. Powered with non-polluting solar power, he has a water-harvesting system and a bio-gas unit, making his house completely self-sustained and eco-friendly. He even grows his own food on the terrace garden.

He has installed a 3KW solar plant that is able to power 11 fans, 25 lights, a refrigerator, 2 computers, a water pump, 2 television sets, a mixer-grinder, a washing machine and an inverter AC. So, a power cut is something that he no longer has to worry about.

Water shortage is common in Chennai, but Mr Suresh does not have to worry about it or pay thousands of rupees on tankers. He has designed and constructed a rainwater harvesting system using layers of pebbles, charcoal and sand in his house where no manual watering is required and his garden always stays lush green.

He considers his biogas plant the best waste management system as he is able to convert all his organic waste and leftover food from his kitchen, garden and even neighbourhood households and use it as raw materials for his biogas plant. His initial cost of Rs 40,000 now fuels his cooking needs without spending for recurrent LPG. This rich manure obtained as a residue from the biogas plant helps him to grow tomatoes, spinach, lemons and ladies' fingers in his terrace garden.

Mr Suresh lives by the motto 'Practice before you preach'. He has implemented green aspects in his house and educates young minds who visit him to take a tour of his house.

262. Fresh from the Rooftop

A supermarket is typically a self-servicing shop offering a wide variety of food, beverages and household products, organised into sections and shelves. It is larger and has a wider selection than a local grocery store. Space is not a problem here. A few supermarkets have taken an initiative to reduce their carbon emissions. They farm on their rooftop and sell the fresh produce in the store below. The crops are grown organically with no pesticides, including seasonal varieties like strawberry, lettuce, cherry tomatoes, and some have even installed beehives on the roof, with the aim of gathering many jars of pure organic honey for sale. These urban farms use water to irrigate the garden from the supermarket's dehumidification system. They also use filtered rainwater.

The crops are harvested in the early morning hours and are on the shelves for customers to pick the early harvest produce. So, this super local food creates the shortest possible supply chain, thus cutting out the food transportation emission which adds a great burden on our environment. These supermarket food farms are the first of their kind, and countries across the world should adopt this model.

263. Smothering Invasive Plants

Parthenium hysterophorus is native to the Americas and an alien species in India, popularly called Congress grass. It arrived as seeds in the 1950s, piggybacking on consignments of grains imported as part of a U.S. government food-assistance programme. The weed was first reported growing on trash heaps in 1956 in Pune, in the state of Maharashtra. It is a highly invasive plant with a history of damaging local ecosystems in more than 20 countries around the world.

Although Parthenium was first spotted in Assam in the 1980s, it had not previously been reported in the core areas of Pobitora National Park, but today the park's core area has an alarming sight: a luxuriant growth of a low, bushy herb with small green leaves and creamy white flowers— Parthenium.

If its spread in Pobitora isn't checked on time, it is believed it could spell trouble for the park's 102 greater one-horned rhinoceroses (Rhinoceros unicornis) by smothering the native species they feed on. Parthenium is just the latest addition to half a dozen invasive plants colonising rhino ranges across Assam, the Indian state that harbours more than two-thirds of the world's one-horned rhino population in four protected areas.

264. Unique Danger

Siam weed and water hyacinth are 'driver species', capable of killing native plants without any assistance from accompanying environmental change. Water hyacinth is the most troublesome aquatic weed which is notorious for clogging water bodies.

Water hyacinth's tough flexible fibre has been applied to create various products such as coaster, basket, hat, fruit tray, handbag, furniture, slippers and purses. So, timely harvesting can reduce the adverse impact.

The invasive Siam weed also shows healing medicinal properties.

Parthenium and Mimosa invisa possess a tremendously competitive ability, known as allelopathy, which inhibits the growth of indigenous plants in areas colonised by these weeds.

Recently, many innovative uses of this notorious plant have been discovered. Parthenium hysterophorus confers many health benefits, namely remedy for skin inflammation, rheumatic pain, diarrhoea, urinary tract infections, dysentery, malaria and neuralgia.

Mimosa is a high-value medicinal plant as it is the source of bioactive for pharmaceuticals.

Ipomoea carnea (pink morning glory) stems form thick mats that block natural water flows. It is also used in traditional medicine.

Mikania micrantha (the 'mile-a-minute' vine) produces around 40,000 seeds every year and colonises forest areas at a rapid pace by choking and smothering grasses and tree saplings. This plant is also used in traditional medicine.

265. Transparent Lake

Lake Baikal in Siberia is the world's largest volume of fresh water. It is so massive that it is known for holding 22% of the world's fresh surface water. With 31,722 km^2 of fresh water, it contains more water than the North American Great Lakes combined. This is the deepest and most ancient lake on the planet, dating back 25-30 million years, and is so renowned for its beauty that it is sometimes referred to as 'The Pearl of Russia'. The water is so clear, that if one drops an object, one can watch it sink for over one minute. One can see everything down to the bottom including fish, green stones, plants, and bluish gulf as it is rich in biodiversity. It is home to more than 2,000 species of plants and animals, two-thirds of which can be found nowhere else in the world. The temperature around the lake ranges from over 40C in summer to -40C in winter.

Winter ice can tolerate vehicles of about 15 tons, but sometimes cars don't have the best of luck, and fall through the cracks. The ice in Baikal is the most transparent in the world!

The lake is situated in a region in which global warming is particularly noticeable. Over the past 50 years, the average surface temperature of Lake Baikal has increased by nearly 1.5°C, and is still rising. The period in winter when the lake is covered with ice has also become much shorter. Despite its listing as a UNESCO World Heritage Site, Lake Baikal continues to come under threat from industrial pollution, agricultural run-off and other environmental problems, including nearby mining activities and potential oil and gas exploration. Since the environmental conditions in Lake Baikal have remained stable for a very long time, these changes are dramatic.

Lake Baikal is a world marvel especially for the locals, and in the interest of preserving our heritage we must all stand united to protect such a precious and unique wonder of this beautiful planet. One such way is to promote ecotourism. Eco tourism offers a stimulus to preserve existing mangrove areas, with the potential to generate income for local inhabitants.

266. Five Good Reasons to Preserve Mangrove Trees

Mangrove forests only grow at tropical and subtropical latitudes near the equator because they cannot withstand freezing temperatures.

The mangrove forests can be recognised by their dense tangle of prop roots that make the trees appear to be standing on stilts above the water. This tangle of roots allows the trees to handle the daily rise and fall of tides, which means that most mangroves get flooded at least twice per day. The roots also slow the movement of tidal waters, causing sediments to settle out of the water and build up the muddy bottom.

Mangrove forests are threatened by climate change and pollution, and local threats. These include overharvesting of wood for fuel and construction, dams and irrigation that reduce the flow of water reaching the forests, as well as overfishing, causing disruption to food chains and fish communities. We are destroying a coastal ecosystem that helps sustain life and livelihoods. Here are five of the many reasons we should be doing much more to preserve mangrove forests.

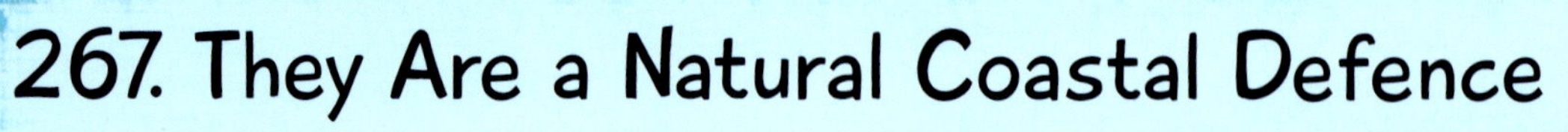

267. They Are a Natural Coastal Defence

The intertwined strong root systems of mangrove trees help form a natural barrier against violent storm surges and floods. River and land sediments are trapped by the roots, which protect coastline areas and slow down erosion. This filtering process also prevents the harmful sediment from reaching coral reefs and seagrass meadows.

268. They Are Carbon Sinks

Coastal forests help the fight against global warming by removing carbon dioxide from the atmosphere, most of which is stored within the plant. When mangrove tree roots, branches and leaves die, they are usually covered by soil, which is then submerged under tidal water, slowing the breakdown of materials and boosting carbon storage.

269. They Provide Livelihoods

The trees are a reliable source of wood for construction and fuel, as they do not rot easily and are resistant to insect attacks. Plant extracts are collected by locals for their medicinal qualities, and the leaves of mangrove trees are often used for animal fodder. The mangrove forest waters provide local fishermen with a rich supply of fish, crabs and shellfish to sell. But overuse has raised concerns about sustainability.

270. They Encourage Ecotourism

The coral reefs and sandy beaches, as well as the forests, provide a rich environment for activities like sports fishing, kayaking and birdwatching tours. Of course, it is important to maintain a balance between visitor numbers and protection of the forests' delicate ecosystem.

271. They Are Rich in Biodiversity

A huge variety of wildlife lives or breeds in the mangrove ecosystem, including numerous fish, crab and shrimp species, molluscs, and mammals like sea turtles. The trees are home to an array of nesting, breeding and migratory birds. When mangrove forests are cleared, valuable habitat is lost, threatening the survival of many species. But that's not the whole story. The forests are also a potential source of undiscovered biological materials that could benefit mankind, such as antibacterial compounds and pest-resistant genes, which are also lost when coastal areas are cleared.

272. Wonders of Prickly Pear!

The prickly pear, or Opuntia, is a cactus plant. It can grow to a height of between five and seven metres and measures up to one metre in diameter.

Prickly pear is not actually related to pears. It looks similar to cactus, with a slightly daunting outer skin. It has plenty of fibre as well as antioxidants, potassium, phosphorus, magnesium, and linoleic acid, making it a nutrient powerhouse. With a sweet, but mellow taste reminiscent of melon, a prickly pear can be used in countless dishes. All parts of this plant are edible and useful, which include the leaves and flowers.

The plant also has medicinal properties to treat issues such as digestive discomfort and viral infections. It has anti-inflammatory qualities, lowers blood sugar levels and cholesterol levels by decreasing the absorption of sugar as well as cholesterol in the stomach and intestine. It is also used for hair and skincare as it slows down skin ageing, eliminates dark under-eye circles and strengthens brittle nails.

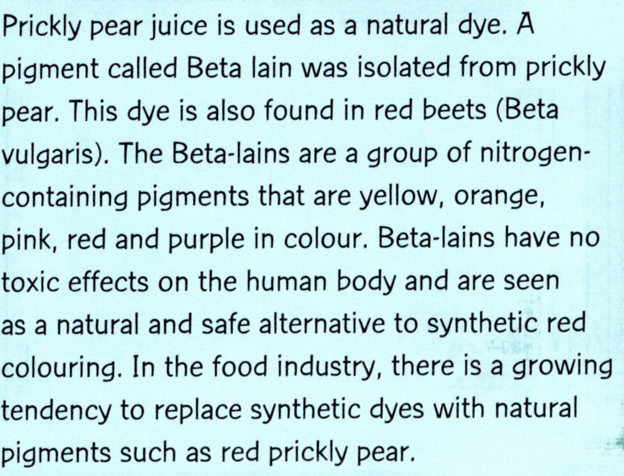

Prickly pear juice is used as a natural dye. A pigment called Beta lain was isolated from prickly pear. This dye is also found in red beets (Beta vulgaris). The Beta-lains are a group of nitrogen-containing pigments that are yellow, orange, pink, red and purple in colour. Beta-lains have no toxic effects on the human body and are seen as a natural and safe alternative to synthetic red colouring. In the food industry, there is a growing tendency to replace synthetic dyes with natural pigments such as red prickly pear.

The prickly pear– known as the Nopal in Mexico – could be the key to unlocking a new and sustainable source of biofuel. A local Mexican company, Nopalimex, is making biofuel from cactus plants, by chopping, pureeing and pulping the flesh, then mixing it with manure and fermenting it. The nopales' flesh breaks down to produce methane and water to produce biofuel, thereby helping reduce regular fuel costs. Its biogas has been powering agricultural machinery since 2016.

273. Promoting Environmental Citizenship in the Age of Consumerism

Change is inevitable. We all know that the environment is dynamic, it's bound to change. We need to preserve the environment in order to meet its needs, in the name of development.

We need to focus on three main aspects that have the greatest impact on climate change: population explosion, technological revolution and the most important one, attitude!

An increase in population has a direct impact on the depletion of natural resources, increasing toxic wastes and pollutants and causing dramatic ecological phenomena.

Technological revolution is seen as an advancement, development, and prosperity, but old habits paired with new technology have dramatically altered consequences.

The third and the most dramatic is our way of thinking, our attitude. attitude. It is so powerful that if we use the right attitude we can still mend our ways, give breathing space to all and save ourselves from the damages we have caused so far to the one and only Earth we have. CO2 levels in the environment have always fluctuated between 170 ppm and 280 ppm for 800,000 years and never crossed the 300 mark. Only since the industrial era when humans started to burn fossil fuels, things changed dramatically!

Nature has already provided us with three natural carbon sinks that suck up and store carbon dioxide from the atmosphere: forest, soil and ocean. Respecting nature and making small but effective differences among all is the need of the hour.

Promoting Environmental Citizenship is the idea that each of us is an integral part of a larger ecosystem and that our future depends on each one of us embracing the challenge and acting responsibly and positively toward our environment. It's about making changes in our daily lives so that we are environmental citizens every day.

274. Extinction Crisis

Established in 1964, the International Union for Conservation of Nature's Red List of Threatened Species has evolved to become the world's most comprehensive information source on the global extinction risk status of animal, fungus and plant species. The IUCN Red List is a critical indicator of the health of the world's biodiversity. Our planet now faces a global extinction crisis never witnessed by humankind. Scientists predict that more than 1 million species are on track for extinction in the coming decades. There are a variety of methods currently being implemented to save endangered species. The most common are the creation of protected areas, captive breeding and reintroduction, conservation legislation, and increased public awareness.

275. Safely Disposing Sharps

Used needles and other sharps are dangerous to people and pets if not disposed of safely because they can injure people and spread infections that cause serious health conditions like Hepatitis B (HBV), Hepatitis C (HCV), and even COVID. Safe sharps disposal is important whether you are at home, at work, at school, travelling, or in other public places. They need to be put in the sharps disposal container and handed for safe disposal. Never dispose them in the household or public trash cans or recycling bins, and never flush them down the toilet.

276. Handling Blood Bags

Blood bags are used for collecting blood donated for transfusing patients. Once rejected for use due to contamination or being in more than the requirement or expired, the bags and any blood will need to be treated before disposal to reduce any potential for infection. Because blood bags are usually made from chlorinated plastic PVC (polyvinyl chloride), they should not be incinerated, due to the generation of dioxins and furans during the burning process. These toxic compounds cause cancers even in low concentrations. In addition, where the incineration devices are basic, the burning bags may leak, which will create a hazard in the vicinity of the incinerator. Small-scale incineration without air pollution control devices may be considered as an interim solution until suitable alternatives have been developed.

World Blood Donor Day takes place on 14 June each year. The aim is to raise global awareness of the need for safe blood and blood products for transfusion, which are significant aspects of care and public health. Throughout the COVID-19 pandemic, despite limited mobility and other challenges, blood donors in many countries have continued to donate blood and plasma to patients who need a transfusion, ensuring a safe and sufficient blood supply during normal and emergency times.

277. Multiuse of IV Drips

Intravenous (IV) fluid drips deliver essential nutrients fluids through a small catheter and tubing directly into the bloodstream. The IV line is attached to a bag of saline solution. The bag is then hung above the patient's head. IV therapy bags are designed to let gravity, as opposed to a syringe or other forced technique, carry fluid into the veins gradually over time.

The used IV catheters can be autoclaved to disinfect them. Then ,they can be reused for drip irrigating plants, especially hanging potted plants as a lot of water is wasted as the water passes through the pot and then falls to the floor below. By using a drip system, one can attach the catheter to a bottle or any water container and control the slow rate of watering, which offers the plants and soil a longer time to absorb the water.

278. 'Green' Christmas

With a little effort and imagination, it is possible to celebrate an eco-friendly Christmas that is not a burden to the planet. You can also help to reduce the environmental impact of the holiday season. Here are some ideas to help celebrate the season while caring for the Earth.

- Think 'Green', buy local, less and smart.
- Choose a live tree or a Christmas tree made of reused or recycled material.
- Choose gifts made from recycled sources.
- Give 'Battery-Free' Gifts, since discarded batteries are an environmental hazard.
- Use environmentally friendly wrapping paper.
- Reuse or recycle gift packing materials.
- Use LED lights for house and Christmas tree lighting as they use up to 95% less energy than larger, traditional holiday bulbs, and last longer.

279. Know Your Waste

Different items like all kinds of plastics, metals, combustible items like papers and rags, etc., should be collected in different bins and segregated at source and nothing should go for deep or shallow burials because now the technology is available to recycle or convert into different usable items. Plastics can be converted into diesel and propane. Metals can be melted and be reused. Combustible items could be used to generate heat and produce electricity. So no more dumping to create mountains or to landfill.

The knowledge for handling, treating and safely disposing waste needs to be disseminated through mass media campaigns, and periodically, experts should hold seminars and symposiums to communicate proactively that as the economy is growing in the country so waste generations are increasing unabated.

Non-biodegradable waste | All types of paper | Biodegradable Waste

280. The Tree of Life

Khejri (Prosopis cineraria, often known as 'The tree of life', has immense significance culturally and economically. It is a small, thorny, irregularly branched, evergreen tree with a thin, open crown. It can grow to about 6.5 metres tall in arid and semi-arid deserts.

This tree has a wide range of uses, being harvested from the wild for food, medicine and various commodities.

- The pods of this tree are used as a vegetable in the dried and green form, rich in protein.
- The sweetish pulp surrounding the seeds can be eaten raw or cooked or dried for later consumption.
- The sweetish bark can be ground and used as flour.
- The plant is used by locals as a remedy for various ailments.
- The ashes of the plant are rubbed over the skin to remove hair.
- The bark is considered to have medicinal properties.
- The seedpod is said to be astringent.
- The tree yields a pale to amber-coloured gum with properties similar to the gum acacias.
- Containing 31% soluble potassium salts, the wood ash may serve as a potash source.
- The wood is used for making boat frames, houses, posts, and tool handles.
- It is excellent fuel, also giving high-quality charcoal.

281. Revive the Lifeline

Khejri, the super desert tree, was the lifeline of the people in western Rajasthan but is now on the decline. The root cause of decline is the indiscriminate cutting of the branches, which takes its toll on the tree, declining water table and increased incidents of parasitic attacks.

The 'tree of life' needs to be saved and propagated widely. It is now being cultivated in arid and semi-arid regions of the tropics and subtropics as an agro-forestry tree, and for soil stabilisation. It has been tested in large-scale trials in Yemen as a drought-resistant tree that can be used as a windbreak against sandstorms. Owing to the deep root system, a mono-layered canopy and the ability to fix atmospheric nitrogen, the tree is compatible with agri-horticultural crops. It boosts the growth and productivity of other plants growing nearby. In addition, it does not compete for moisture with crop plants, which can, therefore, be grown close to its trunk. The trees are planted to stabilise and reforest sand dunes. They can withstand periodic burial by the sand which increases fertility under its canopy.

Propagation:

It germinates best if the hard seed coat is softened first to allow the ingress of water. This can be done by adding a small amount of almost boiling water to the seed (which should cool down quickly enough so that it does not cook the seed!). Then soak the seed for 12 - 24 hours before sowing. Alternatively, carefully abrade an area of the seed coat, being careful not to damage the embryo.

The seeds retain their viability for at least one year, or even decades. The tree reproduces freely by root suckers.

Next time you see a Khejri, nurture it.

282. Stop Talking, Start Doing

The Ugly Indians is a group of anonymous citizens who come together and clean up dirty streets by themselves. Their philosophy can be described simply as: Stop Talking, Start Doing.

They believe in direct action, with a common-sense problem-solving approach. They do not finger-point or blame the system. They believe that there is no magic wand to solve India's civic problems, so, one has to make a change from within.

283. Salute to These

Former fighter pilot Wg Cdr Puneet Sharma is cleaning up his city the 'Swaach Pune, Swachh Bharat' way with his team of volunteers coming from all walks of life. Wg Cdr Puneet Sharma and his team held their first event at Pune railway station on Sunday, 12 October 2014 and ever since, the team has not missed a single Sunday to date.

284. True Warrior!

Sathya Natarajan, a senior manager and executive council member for an MNC in Pune, works by night and is a volunteer by day with 63 different social groups and NGOs around various social causes. He is a national volunteer award finalist spearheading two main campaigns like Pune Tree Act & RED DOT (Dignity of Labour).

285. A True Change-Maker!

'Seed Mother' Rahibai Popere is taking farming back to its roots. She has established a seed bank in her small mud house for the conservation and revival of crop diversity and wild food resources. Over time, many farmers obtained indigenous seeds from her.

286. Unstoppable!

The creator of the popular game Fortnite C is buying thousands of acres of forest to stop it from being cut down.

287. Wise Man!

Pradeep Raheja is an environmentalist at heart. A builder by profession he has dedicated his free time to working tirelessly for any kind of environmental and social cause. He is also a a regular platelet donor. He has been volunteering with the Robin Hood Army (RHA) for the last four years now in Pune.

The RHA is a completely volunteer-based, zero- fund organisation that works to get surplus food from restaurants, ceremonies, parties or any other source to distribute to the less fortunate sections of our society in the cities across India and other countries.

Robin Hood Army's motto is:

* To serve the hungry citizen.

* Stop wastage of food and eradicate hunger.

288. Sipping with Grass Straws

Sadly, a video of a plastic straw being pulled out from the bloody nostril of a turtle went viral on social media, followed by many such videos showing the impact of waste plastics on marine animals. Plastic straws have been shunned by many, but Vietnam popularised an alternative as in the green grass straws that have the potential to truly replace plastic straws on a large scale.

The straws are made from a species of grass from the fields of the Mekong Delta in Vietnam, called Lepironia Articulata.

This grass grows wild in the wetlands of Vietnam, and is long with a hollow stem. These are collected, washed, and uniformly cut into 20cm tubes. The hollow tubes of grass are cleaned inside using a metal rod. They are rinsed again and packaged into bundles using banana leaves. Freshly cut straws can be stored in the refrigerator for up to two weeks and at room temperature for up to a week, if not in use. To make the straws last longer, they are sun dried or baked in the oven and can be stored in the refrigerator for up to six months.

Grass straws are environmentally-friendly and no chemical treatment is involved in the processing. At the same time, they have a mild and pleasant natural fragrance and are 100% biodegradable after use.

289. Tackle Water Shortage Smartly

Due to rising global warming, annual rains are likely to be disturbed. It will become difficult to provide adequate amounts of water to the rising population demand. Awareness is essential for the success of any measure. We all must take into account a deficit rain prediction and plan accordingly. It is our duty to use every drop of water judiciously and recharge our depleting groundwater table with every drop of rainwater falling on our rooftop.

The following measures are a must to fight water shortage:

1. Groundwater recharge using rainwater harvesting methods.

2. Rooftop rainwater harvesting, surface water harvesting, use of recharge pits in storm water drains.

3. Implementation of RWH systems (Rain Water Harvesting) on all infrastructure buildings including hospitals, in the hospitality industry, housing complexes, government and public buildings.

4. Strict water conservation measures like banning of water for swimming pools till monsoon, ban on vehicle washing by water, ward-wise movement to stop water leakages.

5. Switching over to drip irrigation.

6. Recycling and reusing greywater.

290. Vanishing Catch of the Day!

Climate change, urbanisation and industrialisation have hit the fisheries sector in the coastal belt hard with several fish species on the verge of extinction. With an increased number of commercial fishing fleets over a period of time causing over-fishing, studies report that more than two-thirds of the world's fisheries have been overfished or fully harvested and more than one-third are in a state of decline because of factors such as loss of essential fish habitats, pollution and global warming. Apart from depletion of catch, and losing their livelihood, the fishermen are facing serious consequences from climate change, i.e. high intensity winds and waves, coastal soil erosion including cyclonic conditions. These natural hazards are becoming more intense and frequent.

291. Plummeting Insect Numbers

80% of the biomass of insects has disappeared in 25-30 years, a big concern. One of the biggest impacts of insect loss is on the many birds, reptiles, amphibians and fish that eat insects. If this food source is taken away, all these animals will starve to death. Plummeting insect numbers are a huge concern to all of us, for insects are at the heart of every food web, they pollinate the large majority of plant species, keep the soil healthy, recycle nutrients, control pests, and much more. Love them or loathe them, we humans cannot survive without insects. The pitiful state of the declining world's insect populations, including aquatic insects, is due to the role of toxic chemical pesticides and global warming. Other unstudied factors such as light pollution might prove to be significant along with human overpopulation and overconsumption that is driving the eradication of insects.

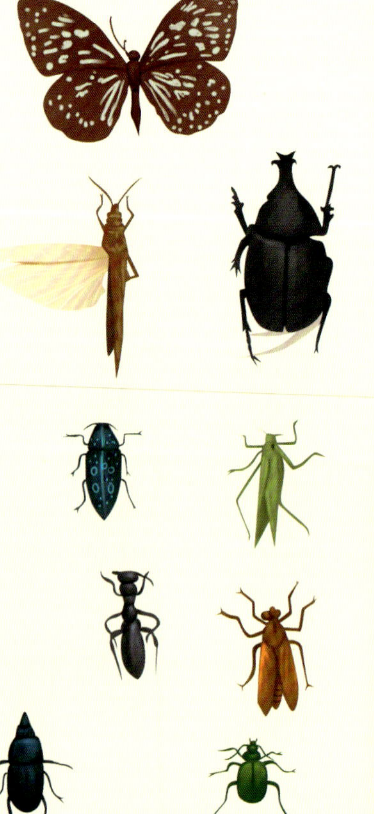

292. Flip-flop

Flip-flops are the most popular footwear that is used globally by all. They account for a troubling percentage of plastic waste that ends up in landfills, and eventually pollutes our oceans. But at the University of California, San Diego, scientists are working to resolve this problem of eradicating tons of plastic waste with biodegradable algae-based flip-flop shoes. The team of researchers formulated polyurethane foams, made from algae oil that are sustainable, consumer-ready and biodegradable. It is high time that we come around to plastic ocean pollution and start to demand sustainable products that can address what has become an environmental disaster.

293. Women Power

A team of mothers and grandmothers patrol the jungles of Indonesia's Sumatra island, on a mission to battle rampant deforestation and wildlife poaching. The unique team of female rangers take on illegal loggers and hunters threatening Sumatran tigers, pangolins and other at-risk wildlife. The women warriors decided to take the rein in their hands and fix the problem when faced with flash floods in 2015, destroying a dozen houses in a community of about 1,000 residents. The floods were repercussions of the mountain being deforested for selfish greed.

294. Magical INK

Solar energy has been one of the cheapest and cleanest sources of energy. Silicon is the basic material used in solar cells. One Australian firm is investing and researching inks that can probably change how we produce low-cost, high-efficient solar cells. Created by the University of Newcastle physicist Professor Paul Dastoor, organic solar cells are electronic inks printed onto sub-millimeter-thin plastic sheets using conventional printers. The tech relies on special solar ink, which conducts electricity that can be printed directly onto the paper-thin, flexible and strong plastic that can be rolled into a tube. This makes the cells affordable and easy to use in any place required.

295. Playing with Dirt

Did you know that lack of serotonin has been linked to depression, anxiety, obsessive compulsive disorder and bipolar problems?

And did you also know that there's a natural antidepressant in soil in the form of a bacteria, mycobacterium vaccae, that is found to stimulate serotonin production, which makes you relaxed and happier? These antidepressant microbes in the soil cause cytokine levels to rise, which results in the production of higher levels of serotonin. Gardeners inhale the bacteria, have topical contact with it, and find it getting into their bloodstreams when there is a cut or other pathway for infection.

Ancient healers may not have known why some natural remedies worked but simply that they did for untold centuries. Many mysteries of medicinal plants and practices previously unknown and yet, still a part of the natural lifecycle, have been unravelled by modern scientists today. They are able to find a positive link between soil microbes and human health, so get out and play in the dirt and improve your mood and your life.

296. Atmospheric Water Generator

Sufficient drinking water has long lacked in the densely populated Gaza Strip. Their aquifers are overused, contaminated by pollutants, degraded by saltwater intrusion, making the water dangerous to drink. By force, they have to switch to expensive imported bottled water. A new project by Watergen has helped to ease the shortage. A brain child of Russian-Israeli billionaire Michael Mirilashvili, the atmospheric water generators are solar-powered to extract potable water straight from the air by capturing humidity and condensing it into water filtered for consumption. Depending on the air humidity they can produce 5,000 to 6,000 liters of drinking water daily, going up to an additional 1,000 liters if the humidity level exceeds 90 percent.

297. Preserve Traditionally

Preservatives are used to increase the shelf life of food and maintain the quality for a longer time.

Natural methods of preservation usually aim to exclude air, moisture, and microorganisms, or to provide environments in which organisms that might cause spoilage cannot survive. These involve boiling, freezing, pasteurising, dehydrating, smoking, pickling, salt, and adding sugar. Sugar is combined with alcohol, and vinegar is also often used as a food preservative.

Artificial way of food preservation is done by nuclear radiation, vacuum packing and hypobaric packing, and the most commonly used method is the use of synthetic chemicals like sodium benzoate, benzoic acid, sodium sorbate, potassium sorbate, sodium nitrite. These are used as antimicrobial agents, inhibiting the growth of bacteria, moulds, insects and other microorganisms.

It has been reported that chemicals that are used as preservatives have side effects. Depending on one's consumption these can vary from very mild to life-threatening.

- Sulphites commonly used in fruit preservation may have side effects in the form of headaches, palpitations, allergies, and even cancer.
- Nitrates and nitrites additives are used as curing agents in meat products. They get converted into nitrous acid when consumed and are suspected of causing stomach cancer.
- Benzoates are used in foods as antimicrobial preservatives, and have been suspected to cause allergies, asthma and skin rashes.
- Sorbates / scorbic acid are added to foods as antimicrobial preservatives. Reactions to sorbates are rare but have included reports of urticaria and contact dermatitis.
- When nuclear radiation is used for preservation it does not make foods radioactive, but may cause changes in food colour or texture.

Stop eating foods that might be problematic as the side effects of these preservatives can be immediate or build up in the body over time and have a serious health impact over the long term. It is best to eat a preservative-free diet if possible.

298. TCD

Plastic has its utility value and has become an essential part of our lives. But it becomes a big hazard for us when 60% of it reaches the landfills and eventually lands up in the oceans.

Instead, waste shredded plastic can be loaded in a heated sealed reactor, Thermo Catalytic Depolymerisation (TCD), to make fuel. Each ton of plastics produces approximately 600 to 650 L of poly fuel, which produces 20 to 25% synthetic gas which gets used in the process. It also produces 5 to 10% moisture, 5 to 10% residual char that can be used as road filler with bitumen.

The produced fuel can be used directly for the burning in kerosene stoves, boilers, furnaces, certain types of gensets, etc. The char produced as the contamination of waste plastic is a non-hazardous waste. Find out the closest TCD plant and send your plastic waste to them for safe and responsible disposal.

299. Intensive Livestock Farming

The popular image of animal farming has been of shepherd boys rounding up cattle feeding in wide-open fields, pastures, grasslands and meadows. Today, the same ranches under wide open skies have been replaced by vast sheds, housing tens of thousands of animals each.

In developing countries around the world, intensive farming is the norm to feed the masses, and other countries are catching up with the trend. The advantage they see over traditional open ranges is the cost to scale, more efficient healthcare for the herds and flocks, and cheaper food.

But the reality is that the increasing number of livestock are 'zero graze', spending all or almost all of their time indoors in large warehouse-type facilities.

To prevent the spreading of infection and diseases, which is a huge risk factor in overcrowded conditions, the factory-farmed animals are regularly pumped with antibiotics in their feed or water. This overuse of antibiotics in intensive farming is contributing to antibiotic resistance in human medicine. If animals cannot remain healthy within the conditions in which they are placed, then it is time to take a closer look at this kind of the farming system that we are opting for.

300. Garbage Café!

The Chhattisgarh Municipal Corporation launched the country's first garbage café in July 2019. It provides free food to the poor and homeless in lieu of plastic waste. Nothing is free in this world. So, what is this scheme? This scheme is being linked to the cleanliness campaign in Ambikapur city, which was selected as the second cleanest city after Indore. The plan is to use plastic for road construction. The first such road in the state has been made in the city by mixing 8 lakh plastic bags. The roads constructed by mixing plastic and asphalt are durable, because the water does permeate through them.

Plastic is a petroleum product and there is now technology available to get back the petrol from these plastics, even single-use plastics. So, treat them as a valuable resource, and not waste.

301. Traditional Zai or Tassa System Overcomes Desertification

Zaï or Tassa is a farming technique. Dig pits 20-30 cm long and deep and 90 cm apart in the soil to catch water and concentrate compost. The technique is traditionally used in western Sahel (Burkina Faso, Niger, Mali) to restore degraded drylands and increase soil fertility. Adopting this labour-intensive traditional technique increases yields by up to 500 per cent if properly executed, as it reactivates biological activities in the soil and eventually leads to an improvement in soil structure, resulting in reduced desertification.

Significance of the Zai or Tassa technique:

- It captures every drop of rainfall and runoff.
- By trapping rainwater, this method increases the amount of water stored in the soil profile.
- It retains moisture and holds water long enough to allow it to percolate into the soil.
- Pits are sometimes dug during the dry season, which alleviates the labour burden for land preparation at the onset of the rains.
- It improves soil fertility in completely barren soils where nothing could grow before.
- It also protects seeds and organic matter against being washed away, in addition to conserving nutrients.

302. Dry Garden

A dry garden is designed to require little or no watering, typically containing soil, rocks, stones and indigenous plants that thrive in natural conditions and the wild. It is literally a copy paste model of the local wildlife flora in one's backyard. To recreate a dry garden that actually depicts the original local wild terrain, one has to recognise and carefully select only the indigenous species and discard the introduced or escape species of plants that have invaded and changed the original topography of most places. Initially the dry garden does need caring and water for nearly two years, but once the trees and plants take root one can gradually wean off and let mother nature take care of the dry garden. It is a wonder to see a wild patch thriving and reflecting the colours of nature with every season while standing tall among manmade structures.

303. Which Country Is This?

For the last 53 years since it gained independence, this country has slowly and steadily managed to find solutions to some of the problems that all countries face. This is a country of many races and cultures, living together in high-rise buildings as neighbours, building a strong racial harmony where the differences are not felt.

Together, they have fixed global problems like traffic by limiting the number of cars on the road, so there are no traffic jams as a majority of people use local public transport. Needless to say, this has curtailed air pollution. The country has also managed to take care of land pollution. The disgusting landfills do not exist as smelly ones here as they burn the trash, filter out the smoke, collect the ashes and dump them underwater in a manmade island, which has been converted into a horticultural paradise.

The country has mastered the art of generating fresh drinking water by building an entire system that converts non-potable water, no, not from streams or rivers, but grey water and black water. Yes, locals take their poop and pee water and turn it into clean water for human consumption. So, if this can be done here then it can be done in the rest of the world, and drinking water will never be a scarce or wasted anywhere.

Yes, the country does have other problems but sharing its success story can help with these problems provided one is willing to change.

We are talking about a small island called Singapore!

304. Rainbow Eucalyptus

Eucalyptus deglupta, or the aptly named Rainbow Eucalyptus, is the most colourful tree in the world. It grows naturally and reaches up to sixty meters in height and nearly two meters in diameter. The trees mainly grow in the Philippines, Indonesia and Papua New Guinea. It is the only species of eucalyptus that is native to the northern hemisphere, and its colours are the brightest. It looks as if from the painter's palette, splashes of colour have been sprayed on the bark. The leaves of the tree are steam distilled to extract the oil which has been traditionally used for oral hygiene, respiratory illnesses, coughs, colds, bronchitis, fungal infections, and skin wounds. The most common purpose for Rainbow Eucalyptus cultivation is pulpwood generation. The wood pulp derived from the tree is the primary ingredient in white paper production.

305. Landfill, Now a Tourist Spot

In 1999, Singapore's Pulau Semakau landfill was established at the cost of $400 million and can hold up to 63 million cubic meters of trash. This landfill is good enough for the country to dispose of trash till 2040 in the most fascinating way. This landfill is actually a resort-like island, a popular tourist spot, with blooming coral reefs and clean waters, and is the world's first ecological offshore landfill where garbage is dumped!

How it works here is that the garbage is turned into ash by the incineration plants and then shipped to the island. The water between the two islands is divided into cells. These cells are drained before the ash fills them. Thereafter, it is covered with soil so that birds and insects can pollinate and nourish the plants. Proper treatment is ensured before the ash-filled water is discharged into the sea, by treating the wastewater which is lined with an impermeable membrane to prevent the harmful substances from leaking into the surrounding waters, thus ensuring all precautions are taken efficiently. This island is a popular bird-watching site as it attracts a lot of rare species of birds and animals.

Singapore's Pulau Semakau landfill has actually turned into an amazing resource-fill, which brings a ray of hope that we might just be able to save the dying ecosystem elsewhere in the world.

306. Don't Trash It. Plate It!

Two professors at the MCM DAV College for Women in Chandigarh along with their team of students won an award in the category for the 'best citizen-led innovation' challenge conducted by the Ministry of Housing and Urban Affairs. They adopted a project that tackles both plastic waste and burning stubble after the harvest, which is a major cause of air pollution. They also emphasise the nutrition needs of rural folk. Oyster mushrooms are edible fungi that are high in proteins and fibre, low in fat and carbohydrates. They are extremely good sources of micronutrients like iron, zinc, magnesium and are rich in B vitamins such as riboflavin (B2), folate (B9), thiamine (B1), pantothenic acid (B5), and niacin (B3). The team's next plan is to fortify the mushrooms to increase their nutritional value for the benefit of rural women. They aim to train local communities in the cultivation of edible fungi by reusing the otherwise pollution-causing trash to empower them financially.

307. Bye-bye Plastic

Indonesia is one of the top polluter sources of plastic bottles, bags and other rubbish, clogging up global sea lanes. It produces more marine plastic pollution than any other country, except China. The solution to this problem is to replace these polluting polymers with bioplastic. Most bioplastics are derived from terrestrial sources related to the food industry, including corn, sugarcane and cassava. The land-based bioplastics require huge investments in land, risking the kind of catastrophic deforestation we're seeing with palm oil. They also use fertilisers and pesticides and are not always as biodegradable as they're touted to be. By contrast, seaweed is cheap to produce as it is cultivated offshore, grows quickly and doesn't require fresh water or chemicals to grow successfully, besides acting as a natural carbon sink and de-acidifying water agent. Start-up Evoware is producing seaweed products that are edible, including jelly glasses, sachets and food wrapping. With citizen movements and attitude changes, it is a matter of time before we say goodbye to plastic and replace its extensive use with bioplastics.

308. When We MIX the Two

What lives in water and dies in water, does not pollute. Fish lives in water: feeds, reproduces, defecates and even dies in water. But this does not pollute the water body nor does it cause any stink. In fact, the fish waste and its carcass become nutrients for other water creatures and life continues to prosper. This is true for all aquatic creatures.

Similarly, what lives on land and dies on land, does not pollute.

A zebra lives on land: feeds, reproduces, defecates and eventually dies, without polluting the environment as its waste and carcass also becomes feed for other land creatures, and eventually turns into humus to fertilise the land. Here too the life processes continue to flourish.

But what happens when we mix the two? If a dead fish is thrown on land and a dead zebra in water, we will most definitely have an adverse effect degrading and polluting the environment as it defies the laws of the natural world.

IF we understand this simple concept.... then half the battle is won!

309. Curb Snake Attacks

Snake bite in the field is not uncommon news. Hundreds of lives get lost due to this. So, the question is how to both protect precious lives without causing any environmental damage?

Bengaluru-based Prasadam Industries have developed a 'snake guard' in the form of a walking stick that most farmers are in a habit to carry for self-defence while venturing into the woods or to the fields. It is made out of iron, and, still in the testing stage, it is being claimed as an ultrasonic, solar-powered, snake-repellent. The device, powered by a solar battery, can work for 24 hours after a charging time of three hours. This innovative snake guard is buried eight inches into the soil where the farmers work, the lower tip sends out 'seismic pulses' every 20-seconds much like stomping our feet on the ground. Snakes and rodents at a distance of 50 meters feel this through their skin, staying away from the device, and the farmer can safely ruffle through the vegetation which is where these reptiles are commonly found. This device not only protects the lives of the farmers from fatal reptile encounters but also helps to avoid the gory killings of snakes by the rural community. It is a minor deterrent compared to the poisonous sprays, powders and sticks people use to keep snakes away or kill them.

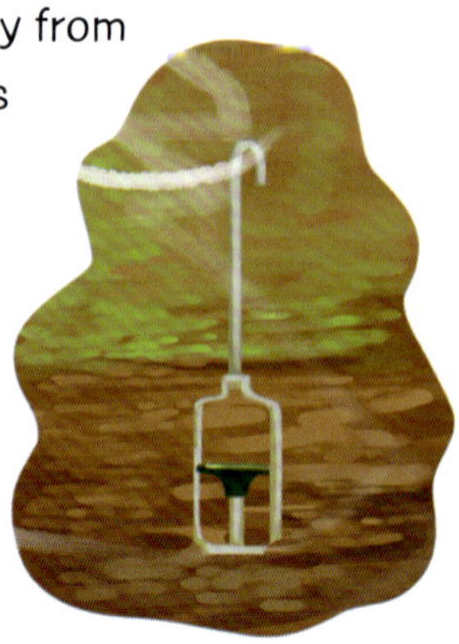

310. The Fire Story of 2020

Early January saw smoke drifts for thousands of miles off Australia's coast. Australia saw a giga-fire during its bushfire season earlier this year. In August, Northern California surpassed 1 million acres burned, the threshold for a giga-fire. It makes the first giga-fire in modern history for California, more than doubling the total acreage burned for the previous record-setting fire. And the deadly forest fires in the Amazon rainforest, have destroyed the home to several million species of insects and animals. The Amazon is considered the lungs of the Earth for its abundant vegetation and biodiversity. Ashes and smoke from the fire spread toxic air in the area, increasing air pollution to an immeasurable level. Climate change is the real reason behind wildland fires and it is urging us to take action to fight for a better environment.

311. Too Many Hurricanes in 2020!

The consequences of global warming impacted many parts of the world, which witnessed 30 named storms from June 1 to November 30, which is the highest ever recorded. The storms formed much earlier in the year than they usually do. The most dramatic was the record-breaking Atlantic Hurricane Season that concluded on November 30. A rare event occurred in the Atlantic when five tropical storm systems were brewing at the same time for only the second time on record on September 14. The last time such an event occurred was nearly half-a-century ago, in September 1971. Among the 30 storms in the Atlantic Ocean this season, 10 showed signs of rapid intensification. Many storms and cyclones also affected other Asian countries, such as cyclones Amphan, Nisarga, Nivar and Burevi in India and African countries, and cyclone Gati in Somalia which brought two years' worth of rains in two days. Global warming is making intense hurricanes more intense and we are nudging up their destructiveness by contributing to heating the planet by burning fossil fuels. We should focus on cutting green house gas emissions to get climate change under control.

312. Eco-friendly Toilets

The Indus Valley civilisation is known for the broad and the sanitised drainage system which was no less than a miracle during those ancient times. But how many people know that the ancient Indians from the Indus Valley civilisation were the first to invent a flush toilet? According to a study by the United Nations, one billion people worldwide still practise "open defecation". The key to solve this overwhelming sanitation woe is to perhaps provide inexpensive alternatives to traditional waste disposal. A few such toilets are SafiChoo toilet, Bio-digester toilet, Ecosan toilet, Tent toilet, Unmanned self-cleaning e-toilet, Two Pit Compost Toilet, The Nano Membrane Toilet, Bamboo toilet, Banka BioLoo, etc.

313. Sustainable Design

In the olden times, our ancestors used local materials of their location to keep their habitats cool or warm depending on their climatic zone, and even constructed elaborate water supply and sewerage systems using traditional and locally available materials that suited the place. Take the Ajanta caves, for example, a series of 29 rock-cut Buddhist Chaityas and Viharas in Maharashtra. The caves have a low ceiling to use the tunnel effect horizontally. The low ceilings allowed the hot air to flow into the cells surrounding the prayer hall on either end, which were filled with cool water. This water cooled the hot air which leads to the cooling down of the entire cave. The stone that the caves are carved into also adds to the cooling of the space.

314. Future of Rammed Earth

A material that is great for reducing the temperature of interior spaces is rammed earth. It is made up of soil, water, and a natural stabiliser (animal urine, animal blood, plant fibres or bitumen). A revived use of ancient materials now uses a new type of rammed earth construction material, transforming traditional rammed earth into the stronger cement-stabilised rammed earth (CSRE) by mixing soil, water, and cement instead, thus improving the material's strength by orders of magnitude. The main ingredient being local soil, CSRE thus crucially reduces the negative effects of transporting other materials. CSRE is also cheaper than many other more common building materials, making it a sustainable option for affordable housing.

315. Break the Monotony!

When the same plant (or plant family) is used in the same soil time and time again, that soil becomes depleted of whatever nutrients that plant likes. The plants get more susceptible to the same diseases and pests that like that particular crop as they linger in the soil, waiting for the next round of feasting. So, to tackle the adversaries related to this monoculture, the growers use more pesticides, fungicides, and other chemicals with their associated economic and environmental costs. But a simple technique of breaking the routine and opting for rotational cropping techniques where different crops are planted sequentially on thc same plot of land, not only improves the soil health, optimises nutrients in the soil, combats pest and weed pressure but also results in highly variable economic and beneficial environmental impacts.

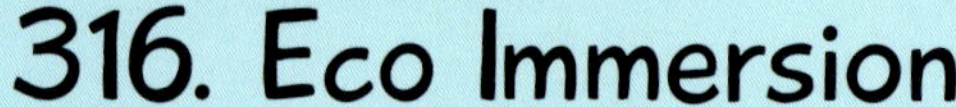

316. Eco Immersion

Broken pieces of mainly PoP idols, strewn around everywhere, is one of the commonest sights one can imagine just after the festivals. These take months to dissolve, leaching out the toxic colours they are painted with, thus polluting the waters and damaging the environment. However, some forward-thinking individuals and organisations are finding ways in which people can celebrate festivals without harming the surroundings, with their innovative ideas. Here's a look at some of them.

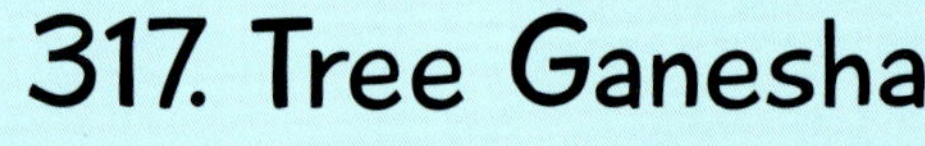

317. Tree Ganesha

Dattadri Kothur, a commercial artist, made eco-friendly Ganesha idols in 2015, which could be watered and turned into a plant. No, it's not a magical idol, but non-baked idols available in different sizes, made of red soil, organic fertiliser, natural colour and filled with either neem, ladyfinger or marigold seeds.

Ganesha continued to live in the plants!

318. Chocolate Ganesha

Rintu Rathod, a Ganesha devotee, would get disturbed at the sight of broken idol pieces, posted on social media as well as the places she visited after idol immersion day. A commercial designer by profession and a baker by choice, she got the brilliant idea of making Ganesha idols with chocolate. There was no difference in the way she prayed to her chocolate Ganesha and when it came to immersion she did it with milk. She then distributed the chocolate milk among underprivileged children as prasada. This eco-humanity-friendly idol definitely puts a smile on children's faces.

319. Fish-friendly Ganesha

Sprouts Environment Trust for the past four years are making hollow, non-baked river clay idols filled with fish-friendly food including dried corn, spinach and chickpea powder, which dissolve very fast when immersed in water.

They reach out to community organisations and schools for children to convince their parents to stop using PoP idols and have workshops to teach women self-help groups to make and sell these idols. They also educate people in immersing permanent idols made of metal or stone into buckets of water so that there is no water pollution.

Now, here's a Ganesha statue even the fish will love!

320. Easy, Green Choices

We can do many things in our homes to play our small part in reducing landfill waste, cleaning the air, saving water and preserving the natural landscape. But we double our efforts when we get our kids involved.

Here are some small, easy, green choices. Pick up the ones you are not doing and make them a daily habit.

1. Plant and nurture something even if it has to be in a pot. Don't give up if it dies, RE-plant.
2. Let the non-degradable waste collect in one corner of your house until it's substantial enough to be sent to the recyclers. Treat these bins as transit resource bins and not waste bins.
3. Remember to reuse first before recycling: smaller carbon footprint.
4. Switch to energy-efficient appliances, even light bulbs.
5. Turn off electrical appliances when not in use. When in sleep mode you are still being charged, switch off from the mains.
6. Unplug unused chargers and appliances.
7. Wash laundry in tap water instead of heated water.
8. Fix leaky faucets. Every drop counts.
9. Go for chemical-free household cleaners. They are safer and healthier.
10. Walk or ride a bike for errands. Healthy exercise.
11. Pay bills online, save a carbon trip!
12. Collect every drop of rainwater wherever it falls to be reused for gardens. Water harvesting is the way forward.
13. Refurbish rather than replace with a new one. Or DONATE.

321. REthink Waste

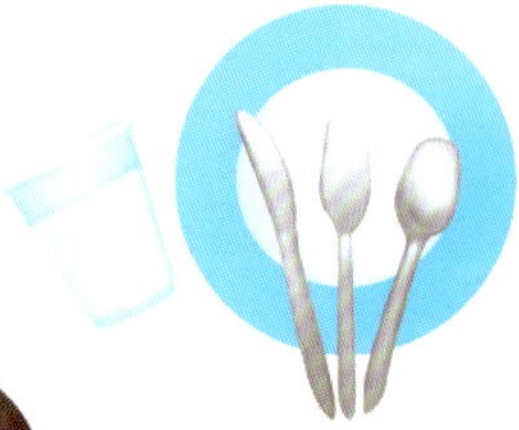

We need to understand a few things when it comes to waste: There is no magical place called 'away' to which we send our waste. Whatever we throw away will go someplace! So, the questions we need to ask ourselves:

• Do the fruits need to be wrapped in plastic, each one separately when every day approximately 8 million pieces of plastic pollution find their way into our oceans? • Do we need another pair of jeans and T-shirt, when from growing the cotton to the dyeing process, it can take an estimated 20,000 litres of water to make just one pair of jeans and one t-shirt? • Do online shopping parcels need to have so much packaging? • Do we need to wrap a gift with shiny plastics? • Do I need to drink with a straw? As many as 8.3 billion plastic straws pollute the world's beaches. • Do parties mean using only disposable crockery? • Do we need to discard perfectly good food into the bin, just because we cannot consume it? 690 million people go to bed on an empty stomach each night.

322. One Shop, One Tree

2Cs that are prominently noticeable in most shopping areas are **Concretisation and Crowd!** Both act towards warming up the place, making it very uncomfortable especially in summers. What if each shop owner has to compulsorily grow a minimum of one tree in front of their shop? So, growing in big pots seems to be a reasonable option and can be placed anywhere. Haven't you seen terrace gardens? Well, the same principle can be applied here too. There are many varieties of trees, and even better if they are fruit trees like guava, papaya, lemon, mango, drumstick, pomegranate, chiku, banana, amla, custard apple, madhu kamini, kachnar, Indian banyan, hibiscus, frangipani, bougainvillea, curry tree, neem, Ashoka tree, magnolia, etc.,that can easily be grown in a large pot. It will not only add to the aesthetic of the place but together will have a positive impact on cooling it too. Spread this idea!

323. Out with the Box!

The first thing in the morning when we get up is to brush our teeth. We squeeze out a little bit of the paste from the tube onto our brush. What about the cardboard box that comes with the toothpaste tube? That's the first thing we throw when we take out the tube. What a waste! Have you ever wondered why it is there in the first place? You know where it is coming from.....Yes, TREES!! There are many companies that package their product with extra packaging, which has no use except, maybe, extra beauty. How about writing a letter to these companies to reduce their carbon emission by not packaging their product with an extra layer which is the first thing that goes into the dustbin?

324. DIY Toothpaste

If you carefully read the ingredients used in your toothpaste, you will come across some chemicals that give the minty froth in your mouth. But what if you don't want to start your day with chemicals in your mouth? Here is an easy way to make your own toothpaste at home. All you need are a few simple ingredients that are easily available in your kitchen. You will need an empty glass jar with a lid, like an old jam bottle. To that, you add one bowl of cold press edible coconut oil and half a bowl of baking soda. To this add 15 to 20 drops of peppermint extract or more, according to taste. Mix them all well. If the coconut oil is in liquid form you may have to refrigerate it for 15 to 20 mins to solidify it like a paste. You can also add salt if you like. First thing in the morning, you can now brush with your own DIY toothpaste and all the ingredients used have health benefits and are totally safe for your teeth.

DIY toothpaste will not only reduce your carbon footprint, but also increase your handprint for taking responsible action.

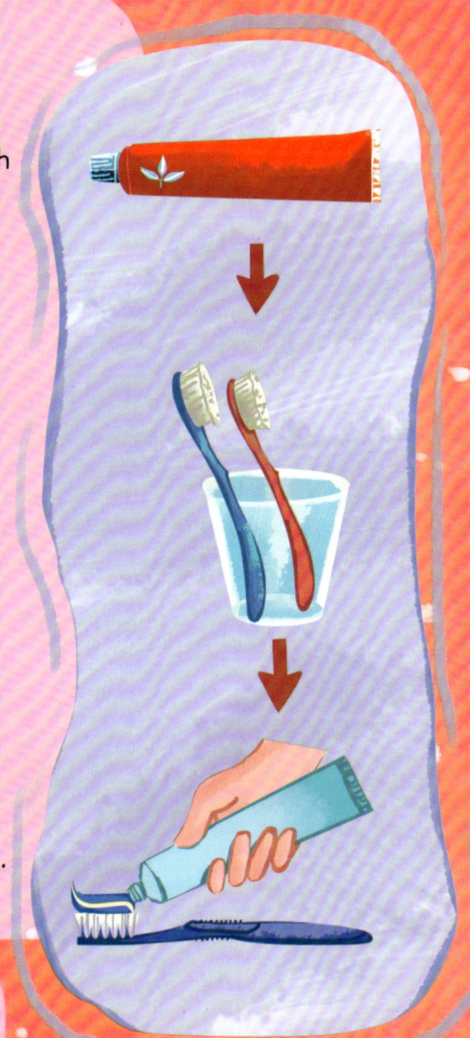

325. Be the Watchdog

The COVID-19 pandemic has seen more and more people admitted to hospitals, where the high infection rate of the virus requires the use of personal protection equipment (PPE), vital for healthcare workers. PPE includes single-use gloves, aprons, gowns, surgical masks, respirators and face protectors in the form of glasses, goggles or face shields. After completing a task, all single-use PPE is discarded using standard infection control precautions. The most effective way to do that is to burn it – high temperatures destroy viruses. Waste labelled as infectious is sent to hazardous incineration plants. Other types of used PPE can be landfilled or burnt in non-hazardous facilities or recycled.

You can encourage the adults in your home to report to authorities if you find open dumping of such hazardous equipment as it becomes a potential risk of spreading the infection.

326. Wet Tissue Mulch

Tissue paper is one thing we use and throw without even thinking about it. For starters, using tissue paper is bad for the environment because it is a single-use paper product. Thousands of trees are cut down and gallons of water are used to manufacture them. When we throw it away, it goes somewhere taking a few years to decompose. So, why not bring it to do some good to nature while sitting there to disintegrate. You can actually crush and gather the used tissue paper into a lump and keep it in the flower pots closer to the stem of the plant. When you water your plants, especially in summers, due to the heat the soil tends to dry up very quickly. But with the presence of this used tissue paper lump in the pot, the tissue not only soaks excess water, but also releases it very slowly keeping the surroundings moist for a longer period. It acts like a mulch. Try it for yourself and see the result.

327. A Fistful of Rice and One Newspaper Roll

Animal rescue homes take care of strays and abandoned ownerless animals, birds and reptiles in need of help. Some offer services of adoption, animal shelter, medical treatment, sterilisation and animal ambulance. Depending on the condition an animal is in, such as injuries or sickness, sometimes they need to be kept in an enclosure, until they recover. These shelters are often visited by animal lovers and volunteers who offer their services to help them out whenever possible. If you are not an animal lover or cannot visit these shelters you can indirectly help out by collecting a fistful of rice and a newspaper roll from your fellow school friends and donate the collection to such shelters. Rice is always welcome, and your collection may take care of a day's feed. The newspaper roll on the other hand is a very handy tool used in these shelters as it acts as an excellent cleaner and an absorbent sheet for animals who are too sick to move, and it keeps them dry.

328. Handy Newspaper

It is good to switch to paperless digital news, but some homes and offices are still hooked to the newspaper. Once you are done with it do not throw it away. Collect it for recycling. You can also reuse newspapers for various household tasks. So, first thing, replace paper towels with newspapers, which is a multi-task master. They are excellent in cleaning glass windows and help prevent streaks on the glass, giving your windows a nice, clear view just like you want. They are efficient absorbent and can deodorise luggage as well as containers. If you have a wet shoe, no problem. The newspapers will do the trick and dry them off in no time. They prevent weeds in the garden bed. Just lay the newspapers where you don't want anything to grow. Newspaper over time will slowly disintegrate and will add carbon nutrient to the soil. If you want to present this book to your friend, gift wrap it with a newspaper and colour it if you like. But say 'No' to plastic wrapping sheets.

329. Small Things Matter!

Small changes made every day can make a big difference when working to reduce your environmental footprint!

1. Enjoy your fruit, but sow the seeds of the fruits to grow.
2. Feed the leftovers on your plate to stray animals.
3. A bowl of water is all that the thirsty birds need.
4. SWITCH IT OFF! No standby. No idle mode of gadgets.
5. Think before you bin..... Reuse-Repurpose before you Recycle.
6. Can't eat! Don't throw.....SHARE!
7. AC and BLANKET, don't go hand in hand.
8. TURN TAPS OFF! Save water.
9. Use sunlight to air your rooms and keep germs out.
10. WALK for your health.

330. Speak Up!

Talking to your friends and family is the single biggest way you can make an impact on climate change. Voicing your concerns is the best way to be heard and also sends a message that you care about the warming world. Social media is a strong platform, so use it effectively, wisely and responsibly. Also find out the representatives your family members have voted for and find out whether they are making decisions that are good for the climate. Write to them to enact new laws that limit carbon emissions and require polluters to pay for the emissions they produce.

331. Wonder Dirt

The lifeless dirt under our feet can have as many as 50,000 species of microscopic organisms living in a single gram of soil. Many of the antibiotics that we use in modern medicine to cure diseases came from compounds found in organisms living in the soil.

Essentially, all life depends upon the soil and it needs to be conserved and protected by implementing some good practices like:

1. Protecting the forest and the soil cover.
2. Creating buffer strips with grass, trees and shrubs.
3. Practicing NO-till farming.
4. Creating fewer concrete surfaces for soil to breathe and allowing water to percolate.
5. Planting windbreak plants composed of shrubs, plants and trees.
6. Terrace planting.
7. Covering the ground with a foliage of trees, shrubs and grass.
8. Mulching
9. Practising NO-dig gardening.
10. Planting local trees and plants.

332. Lighter, Safer, Cheaper

Young Dr Binish Desai has been making value out of waste and paving the way for a greener environment right from the tender age of 12 years. He has developed more than 150 ways to recycle multiple types of industrial waste into useful products, and thereby diverted 1996 metric tonnes of trash from entering landfills. Eco bricks are his main product. These bricks are in comparison to conventional brick three times stronger, twice the size. The most important thing is they are made from waste. In the COVID pandemic, Dr Desai has taken the responsibility to tackle the PPE, gloves and masks wastes which otherwise are polluting our water bodies. So, he made Brick 2.0 which converts medical plastic waste to these bricks which are completely safe and sanitised and can be used to make low cost houses and toilets. He is truly the recycle man of India. So, if you know of someone who is planning to do some construction do share this information with them and others.

333. Webinar – A Way to Go Green

In the comfort of one's home one can virtually connect to anyone, anytime, anywhere in the world, just by a click of a button. The COVID-19 pandemic has exposed most of us to the usefulness of the webinar technology, which did exist, but was used sparingly by a few. Imagine the planning, the effort, the involvement, the cost and the carbon emission of physical conferences and seminars. Now webinars have become a regular communication tool used at work.

You can also use webinars to connect with your friends, make new friends, design new modules to hold educative games, competitions, discussions, etc., and reap its benefits while keeping your carbon footprint down.

334. World's Cheapest Portable Water Filter

Niranjan Karagi invented NirNal, for filtering water. It is a simple device that costs no more than Rs30/-, can be used for up to 100 litres and can easily fit into the mouth of a plastic bottle that is commonly used. By squeezing out the contaminated water passing through the device, it removes 99.99% of disease-causing water contaminants like bacteria and viruses in seconds, thus ensuring safe potable water for all, especially while travelling.

The young engineer once noticed small children drinking water by filling up their plastic water bottles from a potentially unsafe tap. He strongly felt that all children should have access to clean water despite their income or area of residence. So, he decided to solve this crucial social issue and take appropriate action. He researched and used his knowledge to create a simple, affordable device using activated charcoal, filter cloth and a secret compound to invent the cost-effective NirNal.

The social impact of this invention has been significant and has been widely acclaimed for its ingenious and inexpensive technology reaching out to several villages, schools, and even the defence personnel.

335. Cool Cucumber Plastic

Lead researcher Jayeeta Mitra and research scholar Sai Prasanna at the Indian Institute of Technology (IIT), Kharagpur, have made the cool cucumber cooler by using its peel to make an eco-friendly packaging material that is 100% biodegradable. Cucumber peels possess greater cellulose content than any other fruit or vegetable peels. This is a perfect source for food-safe packaging materials. They can be used to pack food, vegetables, fluids or even as waterproof coatings on paper.

The research is still under process and the material is yet to be patented, but it is surely moving towards a positive plastic-free clingfilm world.

336. Five Vegetables in a Single Pot

Gardening is fun, especially if one can grow numerous chemical-free vegetables that require less space and water. There is a way to do multiple layer gardening, where in a pot that is 3 to 4 feet high, one can grow up to five plants of different sizes and properties.

After adding a healthy and natural mix of soil, cocopeat, and compost in the pot, five different plants can occupy different levels, giving maximum benefits. For example:

1. The topmost layer could have tall canopy vegetables and fruit trees like moringa, curry leaves, papaya, etc.
2. Followed by canopy covered vines and creepers like cucumber, ridge gourd, bottle gourd, snake gourd, bitter gourd, etc.
3. The third mid cover layer could consist of fruit-bearing plants like tomatoes, eggplants, lady's fingers, chillies, sweet pea, cluster beans, cauliflower and broccoli.
4. The ground covered vegetables could include all types of leafy vegetables like spinach, fenugreek, lettuce, arugula etc.
5. And finally, the last layer should have underground plants like radish, ginger, carrots, turmeric, garlic, yam, beetroot, potatoes, etc.

337. Make Your Refrigerator More Efficient

To make the fridge work better, certain measures need to be taken that will make the refrigerator more efficient and energy effective.

1. Unplug the fridge and clean the dust over the condenser coils once a year as the main function of these coils is to remove the heat from the unit.
2. Place your refrigerator in a proper cool location away from heat sources as the heat can make the unit work harder to cool your food and waste much energy.
3. Keep the door gasket clean.
4. Declutter, organise and make room for good air.
5. Set the right temperature.
6. Use a power-saving switch.
7. Repair damages immediately.

338. You Have the Power!

We need to stop leaving the lights & gadgets on when not in use, not closing the doors behind after leaving an air-conditioned or heated room, keeping the sleep mode on 24X7. Remember the following things:

- When not in use.... Switch it OFF
- On winter mornings, instead of heaters, sit out and enjoy the SUN; you will get your Vitamin D for strong bones.
- Put on a sweater instead of using a heater.
- Don't wear a pullover and run the air conditioner at minimum temperature.
- Use stairs instead of an elevator whenever possible. The exercise will keep you fit.
- Go for energy-saving appliances.... Start with the bulbs!
- Load up dishwasher and washing machine full, before putting it on.
- Switch over from electric to solar appliances.... Browse and find out more!

339. Poop Charcoal You Can Cook With

A Kenyan startup, Sanivation, operating in East Africa, has combined Kenya's biggest human waste issue and successfully turned it into an environment-friendly, affordable and viable fuel source. They are creating charcoal briquettes out of human faeces that apparently burn longer than charcoal or firewood and also create less smoke and have no smell. They are made through the process of carbonisation, and the waste is left to dry up in the greenhouse for two to three weeks. Then, these charcoal briquettes are heated in a kiln, mixed with sawdust and molasses at 700 C to eliminate the volatile matter and odour.

Literally, this startup is turning man's trash into treasure and saving the planet.

340. Drifting Fruits and Seeds with Plastic Trash

Seeds dispersed by water are contained in light and buoyant fruit, giving them the ability to float. Coconuts are well known for their ability to drift and float on water and often take long voyages to reach the land where they can germinate. But, plastic pollution seeps into the ocean through run-off and even purposeful dumping. A huge culprit is single-use plastics, tossed into the trash or directly into the ocean. Photo degradation breaks the plastics into smaller bits which continuc to break down to micro-plastics and will create nano-plastics thus creating long-term damagc to the environment.

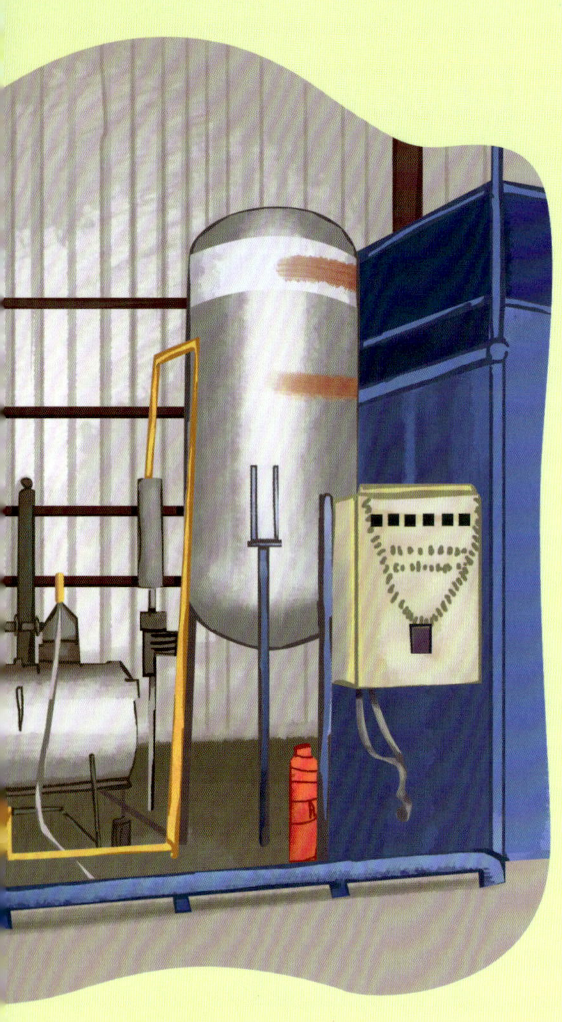

341. Polycrack

Disposing and segregating mixed garbage has always been a massive headache. Not anymore! Polycrack Technology is the world's first patented heterogeneous catalytic process which converts multiple feed stocks into hydrocarbon liquid fuels, gas, carbon and water. The Indian Railways have taken the lead and put in place the country's first Waste-to-Energy plant.

This plant has a closed loop system and does not emit any hazardous pollutants into the atmosphere. Pre-segregation of waste is also not required and the waste collected can be directly fed into the Polycrack plant that is operated at 450 degrees, to be processed and reformed within 24 hours.

The plant can be fed with all types of plastic, petroleum sludge, un-segregated municipal solid waste with moisture up to 50%, E–waste, automobile fluff, organic waste including bamboo, palm, all kinds of garden waste, etc.

342. Rice Husk Furniture

India is the second largest producer of rice in the world. The rice husk is the outer coating on a seed or grain of rice and the residue that is left behind after the rice grains are separated for further processing. These residues are light and occur in large quantities.

A team of four IIT Kharagpur students used this residue to develop an innovative method to process the rice husk with adhesive and chemicals to convert it into durable and sturdy boards. These boards were then used to create beautiful furniture or anything that would otherwise use wood. This type of furniture could help against deforestation and be totally environment-friendly.

343. PH Without a Kit

Most plants have a preference for the degree of acidity or alkalinity of the soil, which is measured by a pH scale that ranges from 0 (extremely acidic) to 14 (extremely alkaline).

If you are a new gardener and don't have a pH kit, but you still want to find out the pH of your garden soil that is suitable for the plants, you can get a rough idea by using two ingredients that are usually available in one's kitchen; baking soda (alkaline substance) and vinegar (acidic substance).

Scoop some garden soil samples from the planting area into a clean plastic container. Add 1/2 cup of water to the soil samples and mix.

- Add 1/2 cup of vinegar to one sample. If the soil shows a visible bubbling or fizzing action, then the soil has an alkaline pH.
- Then, add 1/2 cup of baking soda to another sample. If the soil bubbles or fizzes, the soil is acidic.

The results aren't as precise as a laboratory test, but will give you a ballpark idea of whether your soil is acidic or alkaline and help you select the right plant for your garden.

344. Hybrid vs. Local

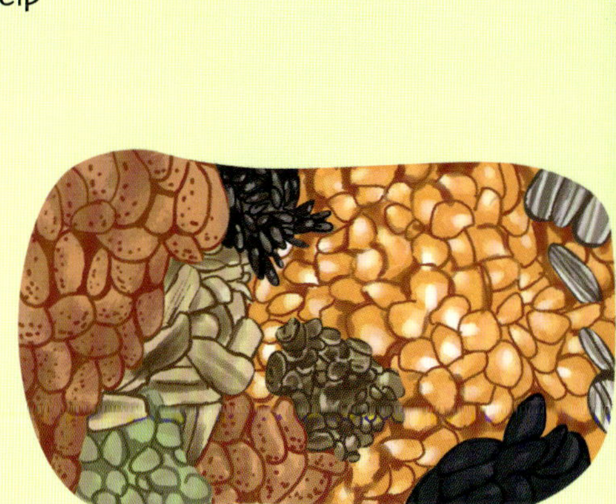

Green Revolution in India's first challenge was to increase the per acre productivity of crops. So, hybrid seeds were introduced to replace the local variant.

Local seeds are naturally carried forward year after year by selecting the best produce from one season and preserving the next season's seed. If you observe the local seed/grain, it is thinner compared to the hybrid seed/grain. In local grains, the seed cover used to be thicker and grain used to be thinner so that naturally it gets protected against viral infection and diseases. Unfortunately, to get the maximum yield from the same area of land, scientists developed hybrid grains to thinly cover thicker grains. As a result, natural protection was lost and produce became vulnerable to viral infection and diseases. To control the same, scientists further introduced a lot of pesticides and fungicides. A trap that our farmers got entangled in when they started using more fertilisers and pesticides.

345. Tree of Life

If trees gave us free Wi-Fi, we wouldn't be holding that axe in our hand! Why don't we value the GIFT of LIFE it gives us?

346. Playing Outdoors

Most studies show that kids who play outside are smarter, happier, more attentive, and less anxious than kids who spend more time indoors. It promotes creativity and imagination. It provides different stimulation and teaches responsibility.

Nature is good for kids' minds as it builds confidence and by letting the children choose how they treat nature they have the power to control their own actions.

347. Survival of the Fittest

With no specific treatment for coconut seed germination, the success rate is pretty high, unless a fractured shell causes the seed interior to get infected with pathogens.

This germinated coconut has survived till now because the white spongy mass and the coconut water inside the shell have provided nutrition and adequate environment to live. But, to continue its life cycle, it has to take root and grow into a coconut palm and for that it requires nutrition from the surrounding soil, which seems to be doubtful in such a polluted area where every inch of the ground is covered with layers and layers of plastic.

348. Trashtag Challenge

Go for Trashtag Challenge. Pick a place filled with litter, clean it up, and post before and after pictures. Ask family, friends, volunteers to join you and make beaches, parks and roads trash-free while also raising awareness of the quantity of plastic litter we produce.

349. Be Aware!

'Out of sight out of mind' does not hold true for burning garbage especially mixed with plastic, as it will go partially out of sight, but the neurotoxic dioxin gases released from burning plastic will surely and slowly poison the mind. Be AWARE!

350. The Power of a Seed

India has set a target of bringing 33 % of its geographical area under forest cover. The forest cover of India in 2019 was 21.67 % of the total geographical area of the country as against 21.54 % in 2017.

As environment citizens we can also help to reach the target of 33%. The solution is very simple and doable. Enjoy the fruits that we eat, compost the peels but do not throw away the seeds, instead sow them all!

Never underestimate the power of a seed..... one day it might grow into a mighty TREE!

351. Be the Change

From filthy beaches and stinking cities to plastic-choked waterways, litter is threatening some of Earth's most beautiful destinations and last remaining wildernesses. This must STOP! Bring the CHANGE and BE THE CHANGE!

352. Drip Irrigation

When irrigating with a hosepipe, 90% of the water evaporates and 10% percolates down to the roots. The reverse happens with DRIP IRRIGATION.

353. Say NO to Food Dumping!

Food wastage is a grave issue. Throwing leftovers into a dust bin is a sheer wastage of resources.

Here are some tips to avoid wastage:

1. First try your best to make what is required to avoid wastage.
2. Give away the leftovers to your friends or people around you.
3. In case the leftovers are a substantial amount, call an NGO, a startup or organisation which is associated with distributing food to needy people and working towards ensuring a 'no-food-waste' future for the country.

354. World Blood Donor Day

World Blood Donor Day takes place on 14 June each year. The aim is to raise global awareness of the need for safe blood and blood products for transfusion.

Throughout the COVID-19 pandemic, despite limited mobility and other challenges, blood donors in many countries have continued to donate blood and plasma to patients who need a transfusion. This extraordinary effort during a time of unprecedented crisis helps save lives.

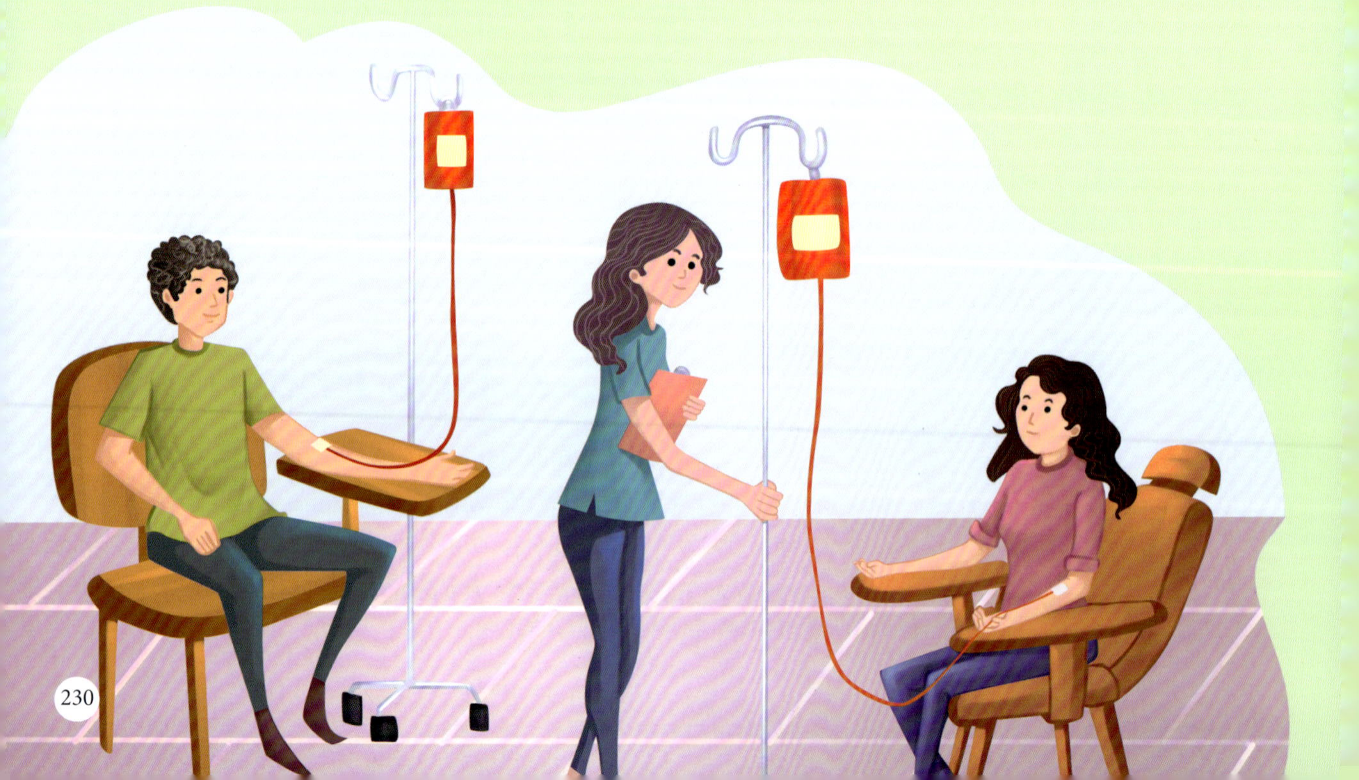

355. Caterpillar 'Plastivores'

Each year, human beings produce about 400 million metric tons of plastic, a number that's set to double in the next 20 years. A way to safely dispose of plastic would be welcome, if only to deal with the plastic we've already created. One solution might be in the use of micro-organisms and insects. A group of around 50 organisms, ranging from bacteria and fungi to bugs, are plastivores, meaning they can eat and digest plastic. The results of an experiment showed that after approximately 12 hours, 100 waxworms consumed 92 milligrams from a standard polyethylene shopping bag. This is a very small amount of plastic that will by no means make a dent in the tons of plastic waste that is produced globally, but it is a promising development. At least we are seeking multiple solutions to a mega problem.

356. Green Swap Groups

If you have a whole lot of old clothes, books, gadgets and other things that you want to dispose of, you might be wondering what to do with your unwanted items. You can always join or create your own trustworthy online SWAP group with your own LOCAL community members that let you Share, Trade, Buy, Swap, Lend, Borrow, Share, Exchange Donate and Reuse goods so you can free up space, make some cash and meet the neighbours.

You can be a part of this culture to reduce our carbon footprint, and make a POSITIVE impact on the environment.

357. Replanting Your Tree

Evergreen trees have been used during winter celebrations for thousands of years. A typical 6-foot-tall Christmas tree takes approximately 5-to-10 years to fully grow. During this growth, the trees absorb CO2 from the atmosphere, helping to offset climate change and global warming. So overall, a real tree really does have less of an impact on the environment than an artificial one. Particularly if your tree is replanted after the holiday season. Rent-a-tree is also available from certain companies that ensure that your tree is removed from the ground and replaced again without damage. But by far the best option is a potted tree which, with care, can be replanted after the festive season and re-used year after year.

358. Adaptability

Water, ice, acids, salts, plants, animals, and changes in temperature are all agents of weathering concrete surfaces. Over time, rain water can seep into cracks and crevices, the seed of a tree may sprout in soil that has collected in a cracked surface. As the roots grow, they widen the cracks, eventually breaking the concrete into pieces. Over time, trees can break apart even large rocks. Even small plants, such as mosses, can enlarge tiny cracks as they grow and survive and make way for others to join in and coexist.

Scientists have found genetic evidence of how some plants adapt to live in unfavourable conditions, a finding that could one day be used to help food crops survive in new or changing environments.

359. Reverse Psychology

"DO NOT" signs often backfire. In spite of several 'NO LITTER' signs and placards on one of Karnataka's beaches there was no relief. On 5 June 2018 artist and sculptor Janardhan Havanje built a creative metal wire fish sculpture called "Yoshi the fish". It was built to raise awareness of the damage caused by plastic materials to marine life. On World Environment Day, over 600 students from various colleges around Udupi participated in a cleanliness drive, which had the theme "Beat Plastic Pollution", and all the plastic waste that was collected on the beach went straight into YOSHI's belly.

Inspired by 'Yoshi the fish', the General Manager of W Bali installed an enormous 'Goby the Fish' on their beachfront, with a signboard saying, 'Goby loves plastic, please feed him!' And the idea took off like a miracle!

360. Power of BUBBLE

Effective bubble barrier curtains could clean up the world's dirtiest rivers! The idea is credited to a startup in Amsterdam. This airy mechanism consists of a tube with holes in it that are positioned at the bottom of the river. By pumping air through the tube, an air bubble curtain is created that forces the plastic in the water to surface up, thus making it more accessible to be collected, removed and sent for recycling. This is most effective when the tubes of the bubble barrier are placed diagonally to the flow of the river. This tactic utilises the power of the river flow to force the trash to the banks of the river, for easier removal.

Along with the plastic clean up, there is a positive component of the bubble barrier curtain, which is that marine life isn't harmed or disturbed, neither does it actually form a physical obstruction to anything passing through it. But this simple device can effectively stop plastic pollution from flowing into the oceans.

361. Solar Leaf

Researchers at the University of Chicago have devised an innovative system capable of transforming the carbon dioxide present in the atmosphere into hydrocarbons. Solar leaf, as it is called, basically behaves like a plant, but instead of converting carbon dioxide into sugar, the 'artificial leaf' provides synthetic gas, a mix of hydrogen and carbon monoxide. This solar gas may be burned directly, or converted into other forms of fuel, like diesel. The benefit is two-fold: obtaining more clean energy while absorbing the CO_2 present in the air.

362. We Never Sweep the Forest Floor

Things grow, die, and go back to the Earth so that the next generation can grow from them. Natural systems work this way. We never sweep the forest floor, where leaf fall is a regular, common phenomenon, a gift that results in returning the nutrients and enrich the forest soil for the living world to continue the circle of life. This technique of natural systems is followed by the Green Manure in agriculture. This process involves growing soil-amending ground-covers with the sole purpose of cutting them down and giving them back to the garden or farmland as green organic matter that eventually decomposes in the soil itself, releasing the nutrients back to be used by the next crop.

363. Selecting the Right Companion

Planting in scattered groupings rather than rows of vegetables in a neat, straight line is a trick that confuses pests, and can act as an 'isolation ward' – one group of plants may be attacked but with a bit of luck the other groups may go undetected! With a straight line of the same plants, pests can simply munch their way across the entire vegetable patch. Finding the right companion and carefully placing the plants, especially vegetables and herbs, have shown to have beneficial effects on one another. Sometimes, this comes down to simple physical reasons – • Taller plants provide shelter from sun and wind for plants that need protection. • Climbing plants can be trained up over taller plants to maximise production in small spaces. • Some plant roots grow to different depths, so simply do not compete with each other for water and nutrients. • Plants in the legume family promote growth in nearby plants with their nitrogen fixing ability. Also, they tend to be deep rooted, which promotes aeration of the soil, thus benefiting their neighbours.

Good plant combinations can help with controlling pests, attracting beneficial insects, filling vertical spaces, and providing fertilisation.

364. Dumbest Environmental Problem

We throw away 40% of the food that we produce with all our resources and hard labour. Along with it, we throw all the energy it takes to grow, raise, ship, refrigerate & package the food too. Collectively the food waste is so much all across the globe that it would have added up to be the world's third largest carbon polluter. Does it have to continue to be this way? Can we not put a STOP to such a wasteful act?

365. Is There No Solution?

There are tons of innovative solutions designed to handle this kind of wasteful attitude of society and feed hungry people at the same time. Are you with us? • There are apps and NGOs that rescue leftover cuisines and collect food from your doorstep and take it to the needy. Google and find the ones nearest to your home. • Bring new technology to food donation. Make sure farms, grocery stores, restaurants near you are aware of these apps and use them to donate the EXCESS food to the food bank in need.

IF these solutions are scaled up, they can help feed millions, reduce excessive resource consumption and eliminate one of the biggest causes of carbon pollution. All we need to do is stop trashing food and our future.

OTHER TITLES IN THIS SERIES

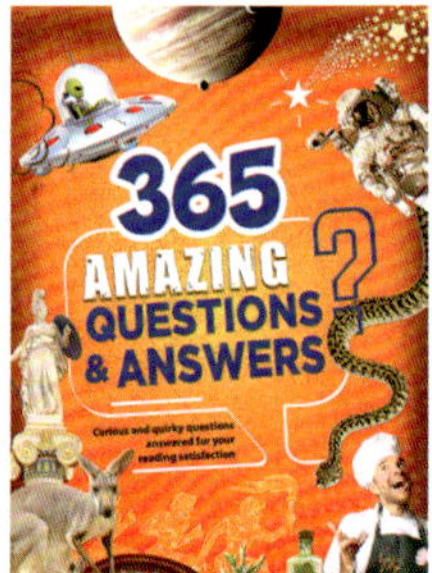

ISBN: 978-93-52760-49-7

ISBN: 978-93-85031-29-8

ISBN: 978-93-83202-81-2

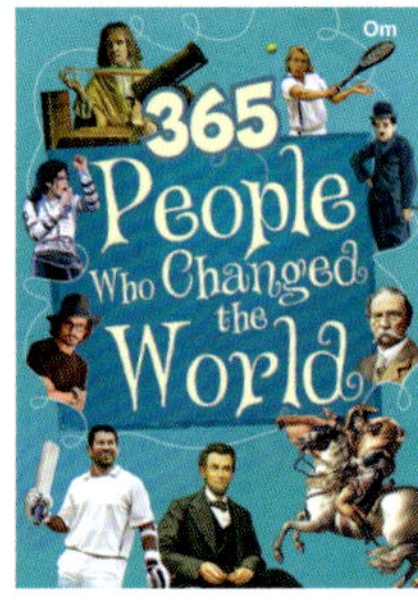

ISBN: 978-93-84225-34-6

ISBN: 978-93-52760-96-1

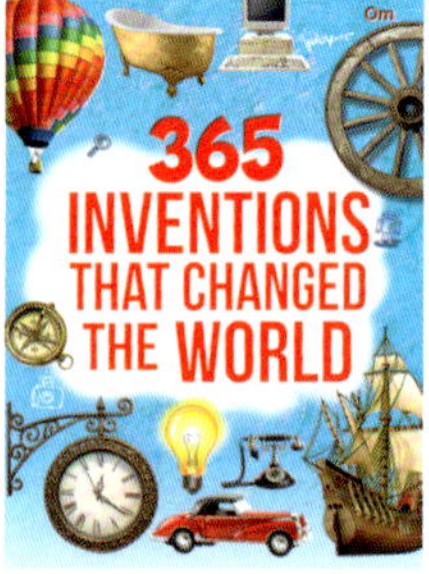

ISBN: 978-93-84625-92-4

ISBN: 978-93-52764-06-8

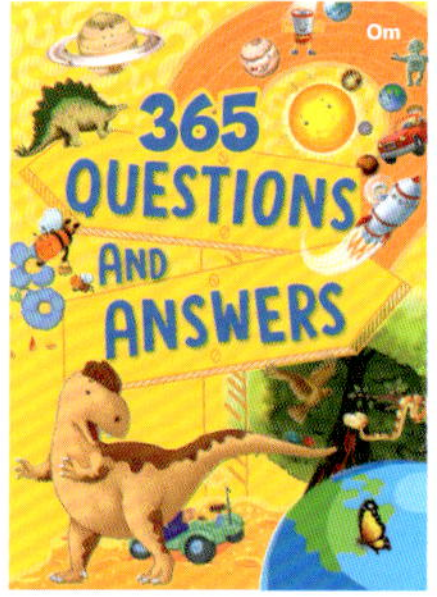

ISBN: 978-93-80070-79-7

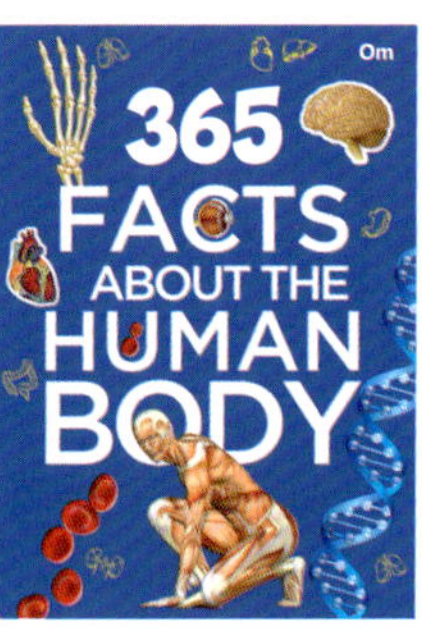

ISBN: 978-93-84625-93-1

ISBN: 978-93-80069-35-7

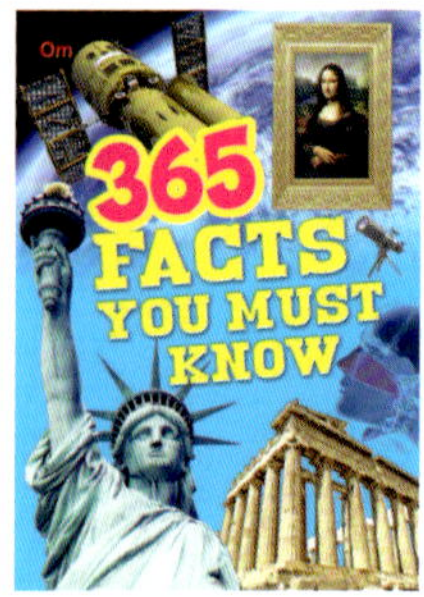

ISBN: 978-93-84225-33-9

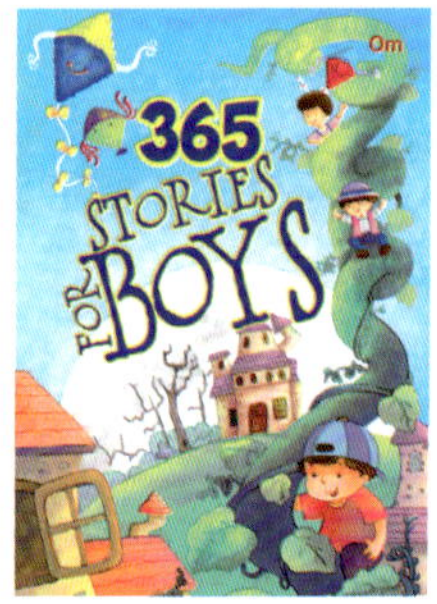

ISBN: 978-93-80070-83-4

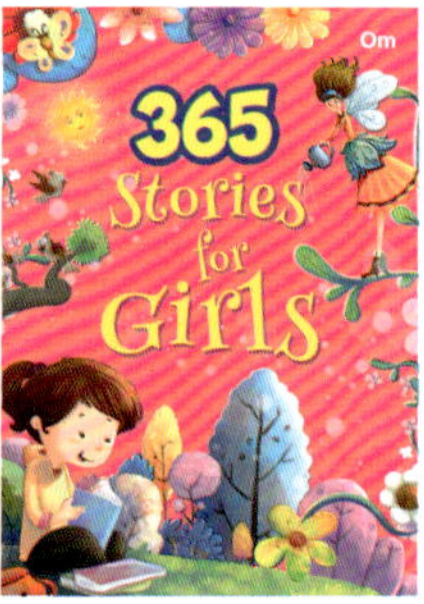

ISBN: 978-93-80070-84-1

ISBN: 978-93-84225-31-5

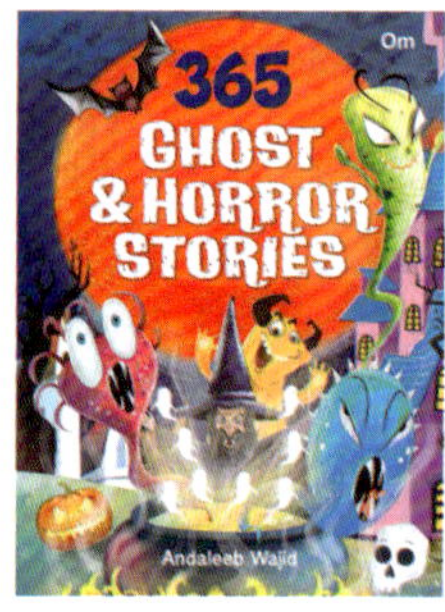

ISBN: 978-93-81607-57-2

ISBN: 978-93-81607-49-7

ISBN: 978-81-87107-55-2

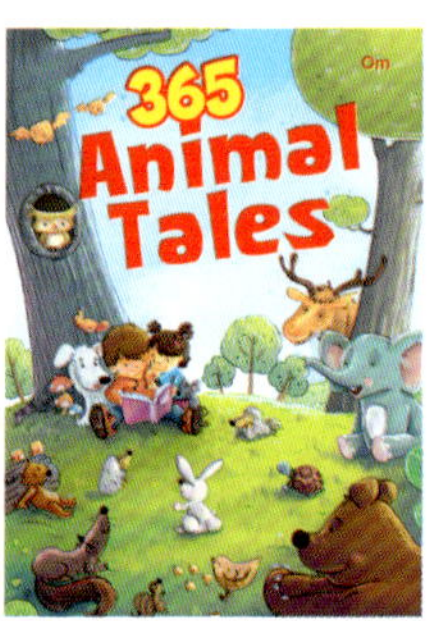

ISBN: 978-81-87107-52-1

ISBN: 978-81-87107-57-6

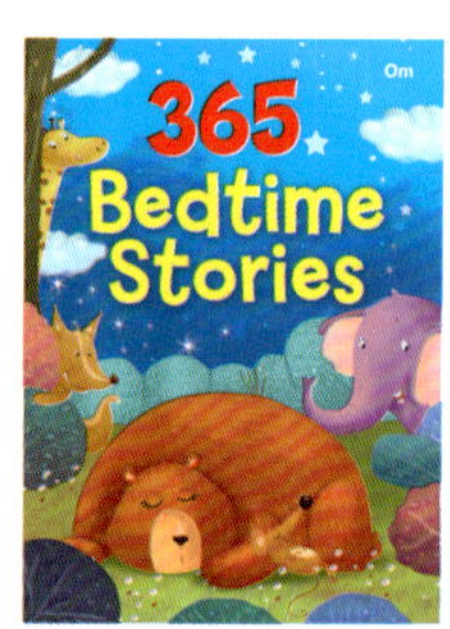

ISBN: 978-81-87107-53-8

ISBN: 978-81-87107-56-9

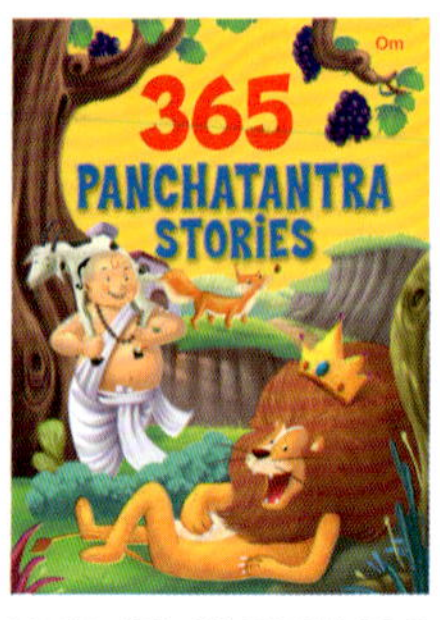

ISBN: 978-81-87107-58-3

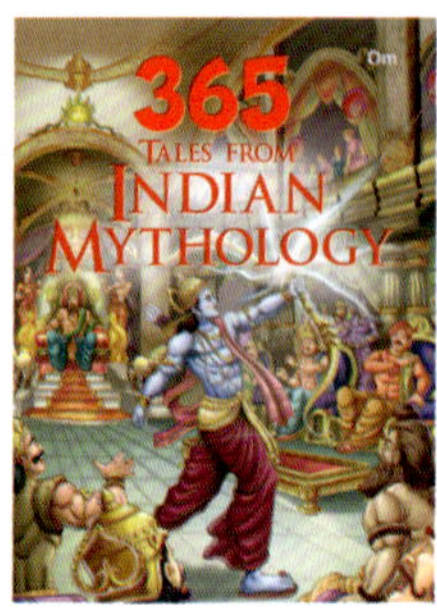

ISBN: 978-81-87107-46-0

ISBN: 978-93-80069-36-4

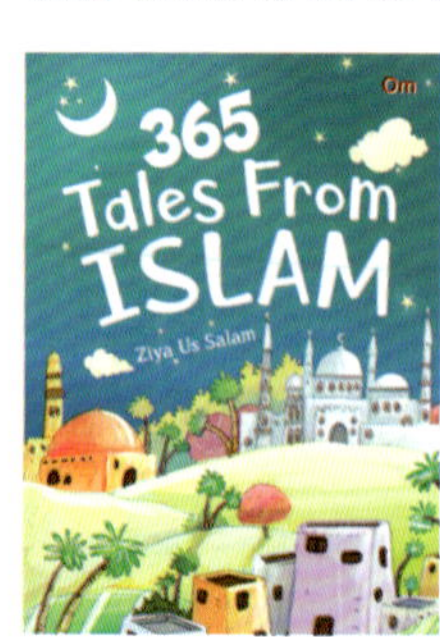

ISBN: 978-93-52764-05-1